Hardcore Love

Getting the Life, Love & Relationship You Want!

D.W. Leonard

4th of July Entertainment, LLC

This book is dedicated with love to:

Noah W. Parden

for loving me unconditionally.

Elodia Peters-Matthews

for being a loving mother and my biggest fan.

Herman Wilson Sr.

for teaching me that everything is funny.

Sadie A. Parden

for making me feel special every moment of my life.

Elijah & Kadar Wilson

for making me a Dad.

Annette-McDonald-Wilson

for helping me become the man I am today.

Mrs. Betty Schultz - 5th Grade Teacher

for seeing my gift before I did.

Acknowledgments

Dr. Jai Cupid – For not letting me quit on myself and for saying, "Hey, you should write your book." Hardcore.

Paul Robinson – For being my ROCK. And for always believing we had something special to offer. My brother.

Johnny Newkirk- For showing me living Brotherhood in action.

Paul Casciano – For giving an upstart kid a living working with the most awesome children in the world.

The Billie Holiday Theater – For being my home for five years.

Sigma Phi Rho Fraternity Incorporated – For teaching me to never quit.

Dwayne Wilson – For introducing me to theater and teaching me to embrace my insanity. I love you, always.

Table of Contents

Hardcore Love!

By

D.W. Leonard

Introduction

ARE YOU IN LOVE WITH YOUR LIFE? Do you awaken every morning, kiss your soul mate, and travel to a career or school that you've dreamt about since you were a kid? Do you work with people that you care about, in an environment that respects your gifts and talents? If this is your life, then give this book to a friend.

If you feel like you're stuck in a dead end relationship, work at a place because it pays the bills or you can't seem to shake the feeling that there has to be something more to life, something better, this book is for you! It is my pleasure to tell you that you are not alone. Thousands of people feel the same way. I was one of them.

I wrote **Hardcore Love** out of personal desperation. My spirit yearned for something, though I didn't know what. Everyday, I felt like I was just going through the motions at home, at the job and back at home. Meeting everyone's expectations but my own. You probably feel or have felt the same way. Like the next twenty years could pass, one day fading into the next, without notice. Without anything meaningful happening. A life without joy.

I was in a bad place. I let the expectations, of those that loved me, influence decisions in my life. Make the choices I avoided. I never spent time caring about me. Never decided what I truly wanted. I shielded myself with the routine of work and let the flow carry me as the years went by. I took on task after task without fully being committed to anything or anyone. I used sex as a reward for not having accomplished anything. I now call this activity, "Filling The Void."

I did not take responsibility for my unhappiness; I blamed others. I made the issue about not being respected at work. I blamed one lover for being a whore, the other for being frigid. I complained about what my spouse didn't understand or didn't give to me. It was all a cover. The truth was, I was afraid to go after what I truly wanted. Fearful of what people would think about me. Scared to shoulder the blame for failure. Deep down, I didn't feel worthy of getting what I desired. At times, I didn't feel worthy of love. Because of this fear, all of my relationships became time bombs. It was only a matter of time until my dissatisfaction with life manifested in my mate, then... BOOM!

I wrote this book because I suspect I'm not alone. It is about improving your relationship with the partner we mistreat and ignore the most, US. How many of us check on the well being of our partner, children, family and job while we pay no attention to our own needs? How many of us are living half lives, not committed to anything and feeling powerless to change things because we fear what others may think?

ALL of our relationships are doomed to fail unless we fix the one that we have with ourselves. This book will help you take an honest look at your life and your loves. Assist you in living a fully present, engaged life. A life in which you can be honest with yourself about what you truly want and how you can feel worthy of getting it. Lives in which you believe and act as if you are first rate, worthy of whatever you deem as good. If you are the girlfriend in-waiting, who dreams of becoming a wife this book is for you. If you are the good guy boyfriend who wants to become a husband, this book is for you. This book is for anyone who has ever dreamt of being more in relationships and doing more with their lives. I am here to tell you that you are a rare gem waiting to be discovered. If you're thinking about giving up, hold on one second longer. You will get everything you desire and more. The most wondrous place in the world is you.

one

What is the Void?

"You are what is missing from your life."
— *D.W. Leonard*

Our relationships don't work, because we're not relating to our partners or ourselves. We use the love that they give us to fill emptiness inside our lives. It is an emotional band-aid on a mental wound. This is "Filling the Void." Let me explain.

Picture "The Void" as your personal Grand Canyon. Now imagine filling it with money, cars, and jewelry. Think about tossing in friends, family, parties and concerts. Picture all the people and belongings, in your life, inside the canyon until it's filled to the top. Suddenly, it disappears. You have to fill it again. Night after night, day after day we continue this exercise, with the same result: Nothing.

The Void is a hole in your mind, specifically your sense of SELF. The reason we feel as though something is missing is because it is. All of our ideas about ourselves are then routed through the hole leaving us feeling frustrated, bored, and miserable about life. So we look for things to fill it, to make ourselves feel better but the good feelings, generated by the things, don't last. So we repeat the process. We are all, in some way, victims of The Void. What most people don't realize is that The Void impacts every area of their lives.

We are all unhappy about something. Some of us believe we need someone to love or life isn't worth living. Others have love, but wonder why he or she is taking so long to propose marriage. Others are married and bored with the routine of kids or a spouse who has gotten out of physical or mental shape.

Even the elderly wonder when they will get grandchildren or when their own children will stop leaning on them and become independent. These situations look like they happen randomly. But all of the feelings of frustration and our reactions to them come straight from our voids.

I once dated a girl, let's call her Sue. The relationship was going well until I got bored and wanted out. I was a player who wanted to date a lot of women so I broke it off. Simple thing, it happens everyday, so I thought. Sue was heartbroken. So much so, she took pills in an attempt to end her life. Thankfully, she didn't. Her actions hit me hard, and though I didn't know it at the time, it was caused by my void.

Several years earlier, in high school, I was tall and pudgy with no sense of fashion, hardly a chick magnet. Girls wanted to be my friend, but not my girlfriend. It created a Void in me that said that I wasn't good enough. Wasn't worthy of love, that my love wasn't valued. No one, it seemed wanted to claim me. This situation helped to form a void in my self-esteem. So, years later, when I encountered Sue, a girl that loved me, I ran. Not because of anything she did or didn't do. Because of my high school experiences, I didn't feel like I deserved it.

When she expressed her feelings, I felt awkward, out of place. I was more comfortable dating women I desired. Once it turned into love, I ran away. Many men, under the disguise of being players, have low love esteem. It scares them. They are not afraid of commitment, which is the popular notion. They lack the ability to process love. If you were told that you were nothing, everyday of your life, how would you treat the person who told you that you were everything? You would think they were lying to you.

People with Voids, all of us, are waiting for completion or happiness from an outside source. Waiting to buy something, to own something or to hear something that makes us feel worthy. The truth is, until we learn to see ourselves with unconditional or "Hardcore Love," we can never be free to be our true selves. We can never be complete.

Abusers have learned to sniff out Voids. Learned to ask questions about hopes, dreams that reveal Void Canyons. And they are more than happy to gain power over us by filling them. When people validate us for looks or talents, real or imagined they fill our void. If their praise falls in line with what we feel about ourselves, deep down, we may find ourselves at their mercy. We come to depend on the Void Filler like a junkie needs a hit.

All of us have voids, which keep us stuck in crap jobs, dead relationships, estranged from family, friends and self. If we don't act to seal them, it can become a lifelong sentence.

two

What Happened to me?

"Pain is your best friend. It lets you know something's wrong."
— *D.W. Leonard*

PAIN is your friend. When something is wrong with your body, the pain let's you know. I call it a friend because the pain signal enables you to respond and thereby heal what is wrong. Voids are painless, but they hurt us in every area of our life. How do we heal when we don't know that something is wrong? While life is rushing by, we don't take the time to feel. In our quiet moments, when nothing is happening, The Void speaks loud and clear. "You're too fat," "You're ugly," "Your parents don't love you," "You better hold on to that man/woman cause you won't find anything better." None of this is the truth.

It's the negative chatterbox in your head. The chatter speaks directly from your void. In order to avoid hearing the voice, we use a host of Void Blockers. Doubt my theory? Take a drive in your car, if you are of age, but don't turn on the radio. Keep your cell phone off. Or better yet, walk around your house without the television on as background noise. You will hear a million things about yourself. Count the negative voices in your mind.

They tell you what you need, don't have, not doing right or not worthy to possess. Do not ignore the chatter, because it's not going away. And replacing it with positive thinking is like trying to stop a Tsunami with a dishrag. We must target the source of your void; reveal it, heal it and seal it.

A New Life! When dealing with our Voids, most of us have the same question, which is, "How did my voids form?" How does something, that I'm not aware of, affect every decision I make? Well, I believe that everyone desires the same thing, which is a good life. One in which they make decisions based upon their values, moving toward whatever they consider good. This process would occur naturally if our baggage, from past experiences, didn't gum up our thinking. I call these negative moments, "Flashpoints."

Flashpoints are experiences from our past that reduced our mental self-concept in such a way that Voids were created or negative spaces in how we feel about ourselves. All of our present and future thinking, as I stated, is routed through this space, sapping us of our power, desire, motivation and self worth. Unable to move forward, from the Flashpoint, we spend the remainder of our lives in a Void Loop, acting out the point of our disappointment over and over, each time with new characters.

Relationship break ups are natural, they happen every day. However, if that break up causes you to feel like you're nothing, unworthy, or leaves you with unanswered questions, it creates a Void. I have seen women fall in love with guys who were jerks. The jerk breaks their heart and they spend the rest of their lives putting themselves in situations where the same type of break up will happen over again. Women often say, "Why do I keep falling for the wrong guy?" I don't think they fall for the wrong guy, but rather they keep falling for the *same* guy, with the hope of getting past that Flashpoint. Their desire is a happy ending. They want their self worth back. Want to be made whole again. These Flashpoints are not limited to break-ups. They happen in all of our love relationships. All of our Relationship Voids must be sealed before we can get our life back. *Hardcore Love* was written in order to help you stop living in the past and find your new life.

three

Holding Your PEA?

(People, Events Activities)

"You can't hide from your voids in the club."
— *D.W. Leonard*

How does it feel when you have to PEA? You start to dance, move, and sway. You'd do almost anything for a release from wherever you are. It's the same with Void Filling, but in this case the PEA stands for People, Events and Activities.

To avoid honestly looking at ourselves, we run to the theater, picnics, the movies, someone's arms, video games, you name it. We practice avoidance of our true selves in favor of someone, something, some event that makes us "feel" better.

Some people try to hide from their voids in the lives of others. They hook onto someone and refuse to let go. They cushion the pain of their lives with the social status, money, and comfort of another, willing to accept whatever treatment the person hands out. When they can no longer fill their life, the truth emerges.

This is because you can't hold back who you are born to be. The natural inclination of your spirit will ring true. It will never be repressed. That longing to do or be something, though you may have no idea what, will not go away. It won't subside until you answer the call. You can't hide from it, as many try, by filling your social calendar. You must search for the answers within. If you allow your mind to get quiet, away from the noise of the world, you will hear it. A Clarion Call to self. To manifest that special gift the creator has placed within all of us. Our spirit.

It has been stated, in many popular books and lectures, that we have a built in GPS that offers feedback as to our course, direction and current state. Wise people guide their lives by this while the unwise ignore or try to medicate themselves (drugs, sex, partying) to avoid hearing it. For all those of you who have cried, in frustration, that you don't know what to do. You do. You're just not listening to the most important person on the planet, you.

Because of the pull from our voids, we have a desperate desire to be recognized as being worthwhile. We want an outside source to love us, to claim us, to praise us for being the best in the world at something. Many of us will do anything to get it. This desperate need takes the form of marriage to a man or woman we aren't crazy about, children when you don't feel the need to procreate and jobs that we hate going to every single morning. We do all this just to be valued. But who determines our true value? We do. Often, the price we set is too low.

I had friends that called themselves players. They spent time with women just to get sex. They often claimed that it was nothing, meaning no big deal. But I noted that this activity occupied a large amount of time. It occurred to me. What is the value of my time? The value I placed on a second could be added up in minutes, hours and a lifetime. So if one second of my life means nothing, the rest of my time holds the same value. How long can one engage in doing nothing before they become nothing? I believe that every second is precious. Too valuable to be used doing anything outside of the spirit in which we were created.

One of my favorite Gurus, Wayne Dyer, calls working within spirit, "Inspired." I was impressed with that definition to the point of ending all of my lectures with that encouragement. We all need to live inspired lives meaning: full of goodness to others, joyful, purpose driven. The alternative is to feel miserable, unappreciated and lost. It is important to understand that, whatever we decide to feel in life, it's our choice and not a product of chance or luck.

Social Void Victims

My cousin, we'll call him Jeff, is the product of a biracial relationship, a black father and white mother. As a teen, he had curly hair and was slightly over-weight compared with boys on his age level. Being the closest of friends, I watched him struggle. He never felt black enough to be black, nor white enough to fit in with the white majority of his small town. So he bounced between both worlds seeking validation through being popular. He had to have the latest car, nicest clothing or be at the hottest party. He made friends with the popular people, tried to date hot girls, with modest success.

Finally, he found his way in via the drug trade. All his so called friends wanted to party, so he became the conduit. I watched him blow through money, cars and women like he was on fire. He bought a Mercedes Benz and a home in a posh section of New Jersey. Still, he wasn't happy. The story ends with two stints in prison for two decades of his life. Why? He is handsome, a gifted artist with a Type A personality. He didn't have to try hard to impress. I now realize, he was trying to fill his void.

In order to quell the pain he felt, the hunger for love, he substituted people, events and activities. It was a cry for help that went unheeded by my aunt, my uncle and myself. I always wondered why he wasn't satisfied with just "US" hanging out, enjoying our friendship. He had to invite half the neighborhood to his house then leave to find something more to get into. Had he faced the boy of two worlds, agreed to love him without condition, he would not have become a victim of the Social Void.

Social Void Victims are scared to death of being alone, so they hide within the crowd. Someone always has to be on the way over, spending the weekend or in a crisis from which only the void filler can save him or her. This process allows them to avoid all silent or sober moments during which self-reflection can occur. They seek to drown out the sound of their chatterbox. I call it being out of their minds to avoid what's in it.

How many women take unfaithful, mean spirited, men to bed just to have a warm body next to them? How many men tolerate frigid, overbearing, women just to say they have someone? How many of us are doing the same thing? This is The Void at work.

The truth is simple. We can't stop our pain by changing our diet, positive thinking or meditation. It will only stop when we are able to fill ourselves up. Until we can look in the mirror and honestly say, "I love you, just as you are." Then we take action toward ourselves that reflects our true value. We can all do it. The Love we seek is inside of us.

The Void cannot be filled. It must be healed. In order to retrieve our personal power, we must face the thing that scares us the most. Our fear. We must face our true self. Our true self is the version of us that is knocking at our heart's door, everyday. It urges us to be and do what was put in us at birth. Until we let the truth of our light shine in this world, we will not be at peace. We will not have the wonderfully abundant joy that we seek.

Why Don't We Just Do It?

The problem is that people do not want to face themselves. To focus on what they truly want would require that they shift their behavior. This is truly frightening to many. "What if other people think I'm ugly, I'm poor or I'm fat?" We make adjustments to ourselves, that we believe, move us closer to who we desire the world to believe we are. The truth is, we are carrying ourselves farther away from the truth of our being. The reason? We are obsessed with what others THINK. Image over personal truth is the path that leads to the heart of The Void.

If my dream is to become a filmmaker, why am I working as a teacher? Paying bills, yes, but also filling a void. I avoid failing because I don't fully commit to being a filmmaker. I don't fail, in the eyes of the public, because I am gainfully employed. If I succeed I take the credit to feed my void. Praise is great Void Filler.

However, if I fail at filmmaking, I can say that I wasn't really pursuing it, or it wasn't my true calling. Do you see the payoff? If we don't commit to our dreams, when they don't become reality, we can claim indifference. We say, "I didn't really want it anyway." By not pursuing our passion, we fail by default. Not trying is the worst type of failure.

Too many of us experience this on a daily basis. We go along to get along, or we listen to people who tell us, "Just do this for the time being," with the promise of doing what you really want, at a later date. Just go along with the program. News flash. Later will never come. The program will never reflect your desires unless it's your program.

If you do not make the effort to do what you love today, tomorrow you will find yourself doing the same. Is that what you want? What do you want? The Law of the Universe dictates that where your mind, attention and energy are placed, you will remain attracting more of the same.

The Problem with Men is...

I've met men who don't fear losing the love of a woman because they believe they never truly gave anything. They claimed they were in it for the sex, housing or money, catering to what they believed to be their egos. They wanted to get all they could while investing very little time and emotion. As stated previously, this scenario does not work.

These men see their interaction with women as nothing, which is really what they believe about themselves. How can a man ever truly be at peace while he believes that he is worthless? A woman placing herself, between a man and his belief that he is "no good" or that she has no real value beyond sex, will always get hurt. Then she mistakenly believes that it is something that she "did" or that all men are all the same. Neither idea is the truth. I've seen women try, in vain, to make Mr. Nothing into something, while trying heal their own broken sense of self. This task is Mission Impossible. This is why many relationships fail to evolve.

By the time the woman becomes exhausted with a man that is taking her nowhere and doing nothing, Mr. Nothing starts to believe in the relationship. Women are often stunned at how persistently they are pursued by the man they've loved for years, after they tell him to get lost. I see you nodding your heads. This is because Mr. Nothing can't forgive the woman for giving up on him just as he realized how much she meant to him.

Truth is, he is no more committed to the woman than his actions said, during the course of the union. This is symbolic of the filling and evaporation present in The Void. The man only understands two sensations, being filled and being emptied. The pleasure of gain or the pain of loss moves people, caught in The Void. The decision to act, based on their true desires, escapes them. Their lack of conviction to act keeps them from living their dreams. Not living their dreams, they seek pleasure in the NOW. To overcome Void Thinking, we must learn to identify our true desires, plan for their appearance, and then act with certainty.

Until we face our fear of abandonment, not being good enough, attractive enough, smart enough, in other words, worthy, we cannot participate fully in a relationship. We will often make a list of traits, about those we claim to love, in order to justify leaving or remaining in our position.

It goes something like this:
List:
Too fat, too skinny, mole on cheek, bald, not enough sex. Great earning potential, cute babies, arm piece.

Of course, this is just an excuse. Simply put, love doesn't have anything to do with your looks or the amount of money you possess. It has everything to do with how you feel about yourself. Repeat this, **"You can't love me, if you don't love you."** You can't give away what you don't have for yourself.

A fractured person will often use self-loathing or self-defeating titles as a badge of honor. "I'm just a bitch, playa for life, I don't love these hoes or I'm too much woman." They hide their fear by avoiding an inner calling that could tell them who they are in truth.

<u>Answer these questions</u>:

1) What do you want?
2) What do you fear?
3) What would you do if you knew you couldn't fail?

four

Caution: Toxic People

"Tell me who your friends are and I'll tell you who you are."
— My Mom

The more you listen to others cry about what's wrong with their lives, the more you will become dissatisfied with your own. You will even make up things to be mad about just so you can join in the conversation.

When we bemoan everything, we are engaging in Void Thinking because we are the ones in control of how we feel. If you don't like the music, change the station. If you don't like your job, do something else.

If we wish to avoid thinking rooted in what we don't have or how unkind life has been to us, we must learn to avoid thinking like and repeatedly interacting with four types of people. These people are Void Thinkers.

COMPLAINERS: For these people, nothing is ever right. Nothing can ever be done to their satisfaction. They could be sitting in a sea of abundance yet they will find the island of want. They complain about everything and everyone. Their favorite topic is what other people have done to them. They have been lied to, cheated on, persecuted by their boss, who is really jealous of their work. They will bend your ear with these stories forever if you let them and that is the problem. A wise person once said that people take on the attributes of people they associate with in a spirit of harmony or sympathy. Complaining is the glue that keeps them stuck in misery.

REPORTERS: Their favorite line is, "Did you hear?" These toxic individuals love to deliver the obituaries of all your friends. Whenever you speak with them they will give you the rundown of who is sick, who is getting divorced and who just died. They will never tell you what's going on with them. But they have the latest on the cheating husband or the wife with the young boyfriend. Why? Is their life not exciting enough? But you will listen and you will share. Problem is, your focus should be on the abundant life and good health you are experiencing. Think of your mind as a magnet. What you think about, you draw to you. If you don't want death and disease, fill your mind with healthy thoughts. Avoid the reporter and their woeful tales.

WHINERS: These toxic people are a smaller version of complainers. Their favorite saying is, "That's not fair." If you think you are always overlooked, underpaid and the waiter always gets your order wrong, that will be your reality. We wasted time filling our minds with a world filled with injustice. Our perception, of this horribly cruel world, becomes your reality through our belief. Did you ever buy a new car? All of a sudden, you see the same model of car everywhere you go. Did everyone buy the same car at once? No, your awareness of that model of car changed. Your perception changed. I believe that life is what you believe it to be. And that Life is just as you PERCEIVE it to be. Fill your mind with visions of a world filled with justice. Perceive that all things go right for you even when they appear to go wrong. Change your mind; change your experience.

VICTIMS: The most dangerous of all the Void Thinkers. They never get a break, never get the job, the love they desire, never get the behavior from their children. They stay in a perpetual loop of how life has done them wrong. They are the most dangerous because this thinking is highly contagious. If you have a friend/co-worker with the victim mentality, cut them off. Avoid them at all cost. Once they start invoking their negative energy, your mind finds their frequency and will start its own tragic loop. No one is a victim unless they choose to be. We may not be able to choose all of life's events, but we can choose our response. We can allow ourselves to be pulled under water or learn to surf baby!

Keep in mind; everyone we invite into our life represents US, to some degree. What we believe to be our self worth. We attract people into our life that will treat us the way we THINK we deserve to be treated. Belief is the most powerful form of thought. If we believe we deserve to be abused, an abuser will show up. Poof! When we believe we are worthy, a caring, loving person will show up.

If you're unhappy, you can change your situation. Believing that you are stuck, keeps you trying to fill the Void. Whatever you believe about yourself, the world will echo. A popular book once asked, "Why Do Bad Things Happen to Good People?" I say it's because they believe it will. We call these things/people into our lives and lament their existence. Control your thoughts; control your life. It's that's simple.

Don't let toxic people talk you into unworthy thoughts about yourself or the world. Believe that life is right. Believe that you are wonderful and deserving. The super model, actress and football player, that you look up to, come from the same place you did. We all spring from the same essence, and to that essence we shall return. Realize that you are not a victim of your past behaviors, rather a beneficiary of the wisdom gained from them. At all times, create positive energy with your thoughts.

five
Void Fillers: Killing Time While Time Kills You.

We use Void Fillers in order to numb the pain of feeling incomplete. Listed below are some of the most popular fillers.

THE FIVE DEADLY VOID FILLERS:
1) SEX
2) FOOD
3) SHOPPING/BUYING
4) RELATIONSHIPS - TOXIC
5) DRUGS

SEX: Is awesome! It is one of the highest forms of energy that people exchange. It's so powerful, new life can flow from it. How can it be bad? It isn't, when used properly. As Void Filler, its power is almost absolute. Moral and religious standpoint aside, the power of sex is in the connection of the individuals. It's a form of communication that's faster and more effective than talking. However, if sex is treated as a tool for release (orgasm) or to get off, it becomes destructive. Like a bad phone call, there is no connection, which is the most important part. The spiritual healing that flows through our sexuality is most powerful when experienced by people joined at the mind. It's the human version of syncing devices or data transmission. Masturbation gives a person the physical release, but without the connection it becomes an empty experience. The energy kicked back into the mind says that I am alone. A more dangerous notion is that people using pornography are mentally connecting themselves to sexual imagery, which further removes them from bonding with people. With that in mind, the number of admitted "Sex Addicts" is not surprising. Any tool, not used for its intended purpose, is dangerous.

Doctors have examined semen and found traces of fluid from the brain within. Those same doctors have studied women and found that, when engaged in sex, a chemical is released that may have properties that mentally bond them to their mates. Let us be mindful of our sexual practice and stop connecting with emptiness.

FOOD: This is probably the most popular Void Filler because everyone can use it. When we don't feel loved, we eat. When we get angry, we eat. When someone breaks up with us, we eat. The "pleasure" of food obscures what we have been denied. It hides the development point we need to reach to become whole. Problem is, all this eating makes us feel worse about ourselves via weight gain and the issues we have remain.

My grandfather used to ask the question, "Do we eat to live or live to eat?" Food is not an issue when your life is a buffet. It's not like those days when we had to hunt or scavenge for food. Nowadays, it's readily available in every corner store. Don't let food be your filler. We must practice expressing what we feel, not repressing it with food.

SHOPPING: When we get upset, many of us hit the malls rather than deal with what's bothering us. A friend of mine used to ask me to hold her credit cards when she was upset. She knew that she couldn't be trusted. Nothing numbs pain like a little retail therapy, right? Again, we get that quick fix. We feel better about ourselves, until the bills arrive.

I knew a woman who bought everything she wanted, only to return it the next day. Still another who, scared of what her hubby would say, hid her newly purchased shoes in the trunk of her car. "What have I done?" becomes the catch phrase. We shop to fill a Void that has nothing to do with what we want or need. It makes us feel good about being…Us. Nice things make us feel successful. Fine clothing makes us look desirable to others. Many think the right outfit will make them worthy. The truth is, you can have that feeling naturally, anytime you want by believing and acting as if it is so. Self-love is free.

RELATIONSHIPS: This is one of the most dangerous of the Void Fillers. Only in mathematics do two halves make a whole. In relationships, it takes two wholes to make a whole. As discussed in previous chapters, it is impossible to fill your void with someone else. To fill our voids, we want our mates to prove that they love us by doing what we desire. In reality, we are asking them to prove to us that we are worth loving, which is impossible. That kind of proof can only come from within. What we should want for others is for them to do what they desire to see in their own lives. Because regardless what people tell us, they will seek their version of happiness. They will always suit themselves.

We must believe we are worth the love of a great person or we simply aren't ready to be in a relationship. It's like trying to fill the Grand Canyon with a teaspoon. Unbalanced relationships will appear to work at first, two people making up for each other's shortcomings, but they will eventually fail. Heal yourself first.

You Down With OPP? – Other Peoples Problems

Many people use other people's DRAMA to fill their lives. They always have the latest gossip on everyone and they are the first to tell you who died or who has cancer or which spouse is cheating on whom, even if they are the person doing it. It will not work. Though we are entertained by the adventures of others, the most important relationship is the one that we foster with ourselves. It is the reason we have such a great interest in gossip, especially the celebrity kind. It helps us avoid thinking about our own life. When someone brings you gossip, ask them what is new and different in his or her life. Watch their eyes for the response. Priceless.

DRUGS: The most deadly of all the fillers. People try to numb the void in hopes of escaping it to an alternate reality. And it works. However, the effects are not lasting. The human body is created in balance. We are naturally centered. Anything that takes us off that center cannot persist. Our built in GPS puts us back on course. The effects are mind blowing, at first, then less and less altering. So the person takes more and more drugs trying to get that initial high.

Eventually, they will burnout or overdose and their journey, in this life, will cease. I watched my brother go from a celebrated actor and college graduate to someone I barely recognized in the street because of the power of narcotics. His void was generated by his failure to accept the fact that he was gay.

Self-rejection acts as a deadly poison on the mind. Accept yourself first, last and always. No matter what your sexual orientation, know that you were created in unconditional love and need never fear rejection.

The Void must be faced. It must be sealed, permanently, for a person to become the best version of himself or herself. The version the creator intended. When I say creator, I mean the energy from which we all came. All of the Five Deadly Fillers have one thing in common. They make us feel better for the moment. For example:

SEX – Makes us feel powerful and desired.

SHOPPING – Increases our self-esteem via the things we own. Nothing that is non-living matters.

FOOD, DRUGS & RELATIONSHIPS – Makes us feel good, though the effects are temporary.

Trying to fill your spirit from an outside source is a fool's errand. We would feel better about us if we dropped the ego and faced who we are meant to be. Say it to yourself right now. "I am perfect as I am." Indeed, you are divine. The missing piece is not missing at all. Find what fills you up from inside and you will have taken a step towards healing your void.

six

Where are my Voids?

"The ways of self are discovered through relationship. Isolation breeds sorrow."
— *Jiddu Krishnamurti*

How many of us use relationships as a tool to discover self? What we believe we are missing, within self, we often seek in the company of others. Many times, we are so engrossed in pleasing our partner, we further obscure who we were born to be. At all times we must ask ourselves, "What am I feeling?" "Why do I feel this way?" With this thought in mind, it would make sense to examine all of our current relationships as extensions of our past encounters. It is all connected. Like a building, the foundation was laid at some time.

The *3 Burning Questions* are designed to shed light on the forces that helped to create our voids. For each of your relationships, answer the three questions and then look closely for patterns.

3 BURNING QUESTIONS:
WHAT DID I GIVE?
WHAT DID I EXPECT?
WHAT DID I RECEIVE?

These areas outline your void. For example: I gave all my love to my father. I expected his time and attention. I wanted validation that I was a good boy, worthy of love. Instead, he was hardly ever around. Many times, he could have chosen to spend time with me, but he did not. It left me feeling unworthy of his love. That void shaped all of my future relationships, especially with men.

I took on friends as father figures, attempting to learn all that I could about the way I should conduct myself in the world. I used women, sexually, to feel like more of a man. I didn't know it at the time, but I was simply trying to fill my void. This also created a Trust Void where I practiced putting friends/lovers on pedestals then knocking them off, at the first sign of disloyalty. Showing them just what my father showed me, that they were not worthy of my time or trust. In my mind, this justified my self-destructive behavior. I was then free to find a new victim.

The truth is, no one can deprive us of anything because we have it all inside of us. We are hard wired to infinite love, abundance and peace of mind. However, we are like cell phones. It does not matter if we are smart, we can't do anything unless we're activated. We have to believe that we are connected to a higher power. Know that we are born of greatness with wonders still to perform, to wax Biblical.

For over a decade, I taught middle school children in one of the roughest parts of Brooklyn, New York. My class would always consist of the "bad" children. Don't get me wrong, I had some very well mannered students too, but the principal knew I was good at building relationships with the ones that had given up.

He knew I would connect with them. I'd make them believe that someone truly cared. I cared. We were kindred spirits. With the boys, many of whom had no father figure in the house, I noticed that they yearned to know about their fathers. The ones that saw dad once a year had a better mental outlook than the ones that never knew the men responsible for their creation.

When my own son was born, I made it a point to tell him all the factors leading up to his birth, how I met him in a dream before he was conceived. How I knew he would become a trusted friend when he became a man. Knowing his origin put him at ease. Telling him about his grandfather and other relatives grounded him, gave him purpose. This is what we must do for our children and do for ourselves. Leave no Voids. Fill them with Love.

If we did this for all children, there would be no need to imprison them as adults. To avoid the pain of not being wanted, children become narcissists, bent on self-destruction. Or they seek to destroy others with the pain they feel from being fractured. Some will argue, spread gossip, fistfight and even murder to try and dull the pain. Who are they truly beating and killing? Themselves. The person not worthy of love, not worth the time it took to create them, not worthy of life. Imagine not being able to swim as the ocean swirls around you.

Imagine the feelings of panic, desperation and fear. The Void often causes people to feel like outcasts in a world of connection or like singles in a world populated by couples.

The great writer/thinker Amos N. Wilson called this the "Nexus of Alienation." Not feeling connected to anything or anyone; these young boys and girls become savage beasts bent on self-destruction by destroying others. However, they are not hopeless monsters. Reconnecting them to their humanity can save them. Someone has to care about them without expecting anything in return. Those individuals are usually educators.

Ask the 3 Burning questions of your relationships with the most significant figures in your life. Your **7 RELATIONSHIP PILLARS,** also known as **EMOTIONAL PILLARS**.

7 RELATIONSHIP PILLARS:
1) PARENTS/GRANDPARENTS
2) SIBLINGS
3) FIRST FRIEND (CHOSEN)
4) RELATIVES
5) FIRST TEACHER
6) FIRST BULLY/NEMESIS
7) FIRST BOYFRIEND/GIRLFRIEND (FIRST LOVE)

PARENTS & GRANDPARENTS: These great parents represent the foundation of unconditional love in your life. They are your parents, but better. Their love is free from the harsh expectations that parents often hold. Grandparents love you for just being alive. They see future generations in your eyes. If you do not get love from this relationship or don't have the opportunity to have a relationship with grandparents, a valuable love outlet is missed. This lack may result in the development of serious trust issues. One may even come to doubt that they are worthy of love at all.

SIBLINGS: Siblings are your first friends. This relationship sets the foundation for the treatment we expect from our friends. How a child will relate to all future friends is formed with our built in friends. If this relationship is abusive, a child learns to conflict with all future friends in a similar manner. Think back to the conflicts that you had with your sister/brother. Match them against the arguments you have with your current friends. Do you see any parallels? Are you arguing over space, property, clothing or attention? Do you submit to what your friends want just to get along or are you the dominant take charge person, like an older sibling to them?

FIRST FRIEND: The chosen one. Look back to the first friend you chose or did they choose you? Look at the treatment you received. Are you getting that same treatment from current friends? Are you the dominant or the submissive? My first friend exploited me, used my stuff, told me things to make me feel bad about myself and finally robbed my house. That made me take a hard look at how I chose people to befriend.

RELATIVES: Are they LOVERS OR USERS? Relatives are important. The interaction you have with them sets the tone for how you will view social groups the rest of your life. When looking at your relatives, think about how they relate to your immediate family. Are they a loving group? There in a minute if you need them? Or are they users who only come around when it is time to fight over grandma's death benefits?

Think about how you view your relatives now. Do you seek them out to share ideas, share life events? Or do you view them as a group that you only tolerate during the holidays? All of this will help to outline your void.

FIRST TEACHER: Before we discuss teachers, let's agree on a definition. Your first teacher is NOT the first person that stood before you in the classroom attempting to "teach" you something. Your first teacher is the first instructor who made you aware of the presence of the divine gift within you.

My first teacher was Mrs. Betty Schultz. She taught fifth grade at Immanuel Lutheran School, in Whitestone, New York. She was a tough, no nonsense, German who took no prisoners when it came to the practice of the English Language Art. In those days, we were called upon to diagram sentences or break them up into their parts of speech. After several of my mates were unsuccessful at diagramming a long sentence, I did it correctly.

Mrs. Schultz beamed a smile that made me feel as if I had won the lottery. She told me that I would be a great writer. Bing! Here I am, just as she said. I love her to this day. My teacher spotted my gift before anyone else, helped me discover my life's purpose. To write, teach and inspire. Great teachers are still performing this invaluable service, for children and adults, today. They are a precious natural resource. Pay them accordingly.

I know that many school districts invest thousands of dollars to educate children against bullying. It has become the rallying cry of parents all over the country. "My child is being bullied. What are you and your staff going to do about it?" We will do what we've always done, which is to speak to the children in an attempt to get them to change their behavior. Of course, we will implement discipline accordingly. However, I feel that there is something deeper at work here.

FIRST BULLY: My first bully was a red headed, African-American, teenager named Eugene. Eugene came around the block everyday to torment me. Once he found me, he punched me into submission. As he beat me, one question played in my mind, "Why?" As he hit me, I would try and talk him out of it, but he wouldn't listen to reason. Eugene would grin as he hit and hit until I curled up into a ball on the ground. Sometimes, my being in the fetal position wouldn't stop him. He would punch me in my leg until all feeling was lost.

The point of my story is not to highlight how evil or cruel Eugene was, rather my response to him. Against a hostile force, my response was to reason, to gain sympathy, finally to submit. All of those tactics failed. One worked. When I stopped showing fear, the beatings became less severe. Eugene would hit me a few times then search my eyes, for tears, for anger because what he really wanted was for me to fear him. He was trying to fill his own void. The cool guys in the neighborhood thought him of as a punk, but from me he believed he could get respect. When I refused to give it, he stopped.

I took the beatings, but I didn't give him control of my feelings. Bullies want to control people through fear and intimidation. They want to control your emotions. Don't let them. Only YOU control how you feel about life. That is one of the greatest lessons I have ever learned. A lesson taught by Dr. King. In this life, we will all take beatings, in one form or another. The only thing that we can control is how it makes us feel, whether we choose to cower in fear, lash out in anger or respond in strength with character and dignity. To beat a bully, one need only remain steadfast in seeing the good and behaving justly toward others. Eugene's beatings helped me to realize that I didn't have to be stronger physically; it was my mental toughness that mattered. I had to stand up for myself. I had to become fearless. That didn't mean I had to punch anyone, but I had to learn NOT to fear a beating. Pain is a part of life. I grew into a six foot seven man who protected smaller people. I would later learn to speak out against injustice. A lesson hammered home by Eugene and other bullies that I encountered. That conflict planted the seeds that would help me grow into a man, with a father in absentia. It added to my life by showing the presence of a void.

Throughout our lives, there will be situations where reason or pleading will not save us. When even total submission will not stop a tormentor or hostile situation. Had I told my mother about Eugene, she would have spoken to him and perhaps the beatings would have stopped. The lesson then would have been, mommy can fix my problems. In my opinion, that is exactly what we are teaching children today. Adults will always be there to save you. They won't. In short, a sadistic, black teen taught me to never surrender. I am thankful.

My intent is not to trivialize a serious issue. Many children, in the face of bullying, end their lives. This has become our focus. I believe our energy would be put to more productive use by getting children to understand courage. Teaching them to fight, mentally. To refuse all bullies access to their soul, their self worth, and sense of being. Not to succumb to the Void of Fear.

To be clear, I am not advocating that we ignore bullying. Frankly, bullying isn't an issue relegated to childhood. Many of us can attest to having had bully supervisors, bully bosses, bully girlfriends/boyfriends. Where will my parents and the school district be when I face these mean spirited tormentors? Will my mother make my belligerent girlfriend or wife leave me alone? Will my old school district show up to suspend a boss who treats me like a piece of crap? Of course the answer is no. Those are conflicts we must deal with as grown women and men. Voids that we must face, but we can fill them by changing our focus. Let us provide all children with positive energy and unconditional love. Teach them to care for each other and themselves. Bullies, in some form, will always exist. Giving children the armor of *Hardcore Love* for themselves and others is the greatest protection that we can provide.

FIRST LOVE: This is the reference point of all the relationships you've experienced throughout your life. It's the reason our marriages and boyfriend/girlfriend-ships are like a rollercoaster ride. We enter them with massive unresolved issues that stem from our first "love" relationship. Humongous Voids we have yet to fill, but we expect the object of our affection to make it better. In essence, we expect them to save us. Needless to say, this is an impossible task. If you have abandonment issues, because of a wayward father, they will manifest in how you relate to your mate. If you have trust issues, your relationship will be rife with suspicion. It's a Void that a thousand compliments cannot fill, that can't be sexed or financed away. It must be healed and sealed before you can be a balanced, loving person.

The reason that the questions and relationships are key in identifying our voids is that we expect from others what we were denied from our Emotional Pillars. Until the Love Relationship Void is filled, we are doomed to replay our first failed relationship over and over again with new friends, family and mates.

This is why divorce isn't always effective in solving marital woes. As a wise person once stated, "Wherever you go, there you are." You carry yourself into the new relationship. The new mate becomes the old. Maybe, it's peaceful, different for a time, until your voids become active. Why can't we escape? Simple. You cannot expect to receive from someone, what you are not willing to give yourself. We must identify, heal and seal our voids in order to give and receive Unconditional Love.

One of the worst things a person can do is to create a child in hopes of filling their void. People mistakenly believe that having children can fix their Void ridden relationships or to cement them to their mates. Children can't fill a void. They look to you to show them how to fill themselves up. Let me say that again. If you raise a child in Hardcore Love, they will have no voids to fill. The child will be fearless, bold, daring yet humble, loving and mannerly.

How many children have you met like this? We have a society that has fallen victim to The Void, like the great plague back in medieval times. It is a creeping dissatisfaction that sucks away life's joy. But we can get it all back. We can seal our voids, live as nature intended, freely, abundantly and without fear.

OUR WORDS & THE VOIDS THEY CREATE IN CHILDREN:
YOU ARE STUPID - LOW SELF ESTEEM (MENTAL)
YOU ARE UGLY - LOW SELF ESTEEM (PHYSICAL)
YOU ARE TALENT LESS - AFRAID TO TRY ANYTHING
I DON'T WANT YOU - ABANDONMENT/TRUST ISSUES
YOU ARE JUST LIKE YOUR NO GOOD
FATHER/MOTHER - SELF HATRED

If you tell a child any of these things, in words or actions, you create a Void in their sense of self. Sadly, those seeking to abuse or exploit them often fill it.

Michael Jackson is the King of Pop Music. He was the greatest entertainer to ever grace a stage. Perhaps, the biggest star on the planet, even in death. By accounts from those closest to him, his void wasn't filled in several areas. His father called him "Big nose," according to reports; Michael believed that his nose made him unattractive. He was also sensitive to a progressive skin condition. Subsequently, he endured millions of dollars worth of plastic surgery, countless hours of skin bleaching and was painfully insecure.

During an interview, Michael stated that he felt most connected to his power when he was on stage. Entertaining the masses of the people brought him joy. Rather then engage with insincere talk with adults that admired him for his fame, he chose the unconditional love of children. Michael worked a grueling schedule in order to fill his void, in order to not let down the fans, people whom he truly loved. Finally he turned to drugs, to aid him in sleeping, which proved fatal. Had Michael been able to identify and address his voids, much of his suffering could have been halted. You now have the ability to identify your voids. The choice of whether or not to face them is yours. Do not wait until it is too late.

seven

Modern Relationships

"If one is not on their life purpose, a relationship is impossible."
-D.W. Leonard

"He just doesn't understand me!" I've heard it a million times, so have you. We suffer in modern relationships because we don't understand each other. We are not on the same page. We look to others for our happiness, when we should be looking at ourselves.

Absent your children, your spouse and your miscellaneous obligations, what fills you up on the inside? What makes your toes curl about yourself? Only you know that one thing that can snap you out of mental, physical or spiritual inertia. It is the one thing that causes you to vibrate at your highest level. Makes you happy and joyful. You don't have to go out and get it. It's part of you.

You must determine exactly what you want from this life. You must be honest and face your fears. Write down your dreams, your plans; say them to yourself every night before you go to bed and every morning when you awake. Self Love cannot occur without being honest. Because we do not love ourselves, as we should, our voids cause a cycle I call the **5 STAGES OF MODERN RELATIONSHIPS**. Undoubtedly, you have experienced one stage or all of them, first hand.

5 STAGES OF MODERN RELATIONSHIPS
1. THE MEETING - Voids Hidden/Requirements
2. OXYGEN PHASE - Perfect - Can't get enough of them.

3. DECAY - Enthusiasm/Excitement decreases - Voids
4. THE BATTLE - Resentment/ Get back to Oxygen.
5. THE BREAK UP – One or both want out.

THE MEETING:

During the Meeting Stage, many times we are focused on finding a person to fill our void. To expose our needs, too early, would scare away potential fillers. So we become a less intense version of ourselves. We are happy with everything and nothing is an issue. "It's cool," should be the catch phrase for this time. We are trying to catch someone with our ideal self.

Realize that you can never obscure who you are, completely. The fun, easygoing, non-judgmental person is part of you. The person, who cares about others, enjoys movies and a dog is all you. You just hide your expectations. It's your baggage. Once we have healed our voids, the Meeting Stage takes on new meaning.

The meeting isn't to see if we can "hook up" or find out who is qualified for marriage. A Void Free Meeting is an invitation to walk together. Friendship. No requirements, no expectations. What's given is good energy, nothing more, nothing less. Physical features and social status do not enter the equation, for those are requirements of the Void. Physical intimacy is not the focus. It's just a walk. If you get the sense that the other person has agendas or plans that do not jibe with yours, you may choose to discontinue your walk. Simple.

THE OXYGEN PHASE:

This is my favorite part of the relationship. How could you not love it? Everything is brand new. No one has screwed up yet. This part is celebrated in movies, popularized by novels. It is a time during which romantic notions sweep us off our feet. When the object of our affection can, literally, do no wrong. Hours spent on the phone, with the last half hour dedicated to who should hang up first. If only it could last forever.

During this stage, we waive all of our rights to know about each other's voids. We know there is something there. We might even catch glimpses of irrational behavior or insecurity, but who cares. We are in heavy like. It would be foolish of me, or anyone else, to talk you out of being in this awesome state. However, I would suggest caution.

Use the energy of the Oxygen Phase, the mighty power it bestows to gather information. Use the fearlessness to ask questions. Probe your new friend. Talk to his/her friends, family and their exes. A wise person once said,

"The beginning is the ending." The misstep many of us take it thinking the person will somehow be transformed in the process of knowing us.

Truth is, the process of relationship exposes who we are. It does not improve our character unless that is our desire. Also, anything agreed to, during the meeting phase, will be the standard for the remainder of the union unless drastic action is taken. Under no circumstances should one consent to an off the books or non-public relationship unless they would like to be kept a secret for the ENTIRE union. Make certain that you're allowed full access to all family members, home phone numbers, homes and friends.

DECAY: This is the least enjoyable part of any relationship. We have become so comfortable we finally let our mates see our voids. Slowly at first, but then... Separation issues, contact issues, abandonment issues, residue of child abuse, trust issues appear. It's love me or leave me time, but no matter how bad the person's issues appear, we hang in there. WE believe, as a child, that this will blow over and things will be as they were. Like a drug, the Oxygen Phase was so good that we want another hit. We know it's there, under all the muck and mire. If we just love them hard enough, the person we grew to love will show up again. All will be well.

I knew a woman who thought she had the perfect man, next thing you know he was stalking her in clubs, camping out in front of her house and sniffing her underwear to see if she was being unfaithful. She didn't see that his void was his weak self-esteem and that he was riddled with abandonment issues till it was too late. In truth, it was there all the time.

THE BATTLE: The battle is the struggle to get back to the Oxygen Phase. Get back to the time when everything seemed to just flow minus the heavy hang-ups. So we look to our mates to understand. "You know how I am," could be the catch phrase. But as previously stated, it's just not the same and never will be.

THE BREAK UP: One of you has had enough of misunderstanding the other's void and is ready to call it quits. A few parting shots, then you are off to discover life with the next person. However, if you don't take the time to seal your void, the cycle will just repeat itself. Why? Our attempts fail because we don't understand the issue. We misunderstand our voids and expect others to fill them. However, Voids can only be healed from WITHIN.

I don't mean to be cruel, but it is the Law of the Universe. You can't give away what you don't have for yourself. You can't Love me if you don't Love yourself. That means all parts of you. Your height, weight, speech, your nose, whatever. Don't reject it, because that is rejecting you. Say it; realize it. "I am in LOVE with every part of myself. It's all me and it's all good." Smile then hug yourself really hard.

Write out that positive affirmation, place it somewhere you can see it everyday. Repeat the self-love message to yourself then act in ways that enforce it. I knew a woman who, without a mate, took herself out to dinner at her favorite restaurant then to a movie, finally home for a warm candlelit bath and soothing music. How many of us take ourselves on dates? What better company is there?

Love yourself, and then act in ways that you would want a future partner to treat you. You will be amazed how quickly that partner arrives and treats you just as you've always dreamt she/he would. All relationships are rooted in the one that we have with ourselves. Make it extraordinary.

eight
Ghost Relationships

"Your relationships don't fail, they stop evolving."
— D.W. Leonard

Most of us are NOT satisfied by the work we do or by the girlfriend, boyfriend or spouse we have chosen. Those of us who gain money find out that, while nice, it does not guarantee your happiness. In fact, money often adds to an individual's confusion about the meaning of life. The satisfaction of things is temporary, while a true sense of joy eludes us.

We live in a technological age where everything is possible in an instant. We can video chat with people across the globe from a device that fits in the palm of our hand. Yet people take drugs for loneliness and depression at a higher rate than ever before. We often ignore family members for years at a time. We live with the persistent feeling that something is missing. What could it be? Something inside us clamors for more. More what?

Once upon a time, I believed that relationships happened by chance. That love was a happy accident. Greeting cards make millions from this notion. It is a wonderful sentiment albeit a tad off the mark. It appears as if there is a meeting, two people hit it off. Love, sex, marriage and children follow. The belief that we have little to no control of the ritual has also been popularized. There is nothing you can do when you "fall" in love. We believe that we have no control over whom we attract or to whom we are attracted. Stuff "just happens." To put it simply, that's a load of crap.

The truth is, we call people into our lives. Our relationships are opportunities to discover the truth about us. To give us the chance to see what we are truly made of, afraid of, and ashamed of. Our chance to get it out into the open and put it to rest, once and for all. The mind doesn't like loose ends so it provides us with opportunities to resolve them through relationships.

All of our lives, we are trying to heal wounds suffered in our childhood and adolescence. To make everything all right for a little boy or girl that no longer exists. The truth is, we are still that crying child being teased on the playground, the overweight kid in the class, the "ugly" that didn't get asked to the prom. We try to void fill the present to keep from living in the past.

For those of us who didn't have the approval of our mother/father as a child, we spend life trying to show them that we are worthy, even when they are deceased. For those of us who were thought of as not cute, we spend life dressing and preening to get attention. Whatever spot in our mind, our sense of self that was not reinforced by Hardcore Love we seek people, events, activities or things to fill it. It is like consuming junk food to stop your hunger. It fills you up, but with no nutritional value, so it ends up weighing you down. But there is hope. You can heal and seal your void. The trick is, knowing what it is. If you're still unsure, do this quick exercise. Utilize the 3 VOID PROBES.

3 VOID PROBES:

1) IN RELATIONSHIPS, WHAT DO YOU EXPECT BUT DON'T RECEIVE?

2) WHAT DID YOUR EMOTIONAL PILLARS DO THAT STILL HURTS?

3) WHAT DON'T YOU LIKE ABOUT YOURSELF? (Mentally/ Physically)

In my case, the answer to the first two is time and attention. I didn't receive it, so I don't give it. If you ask any of the women I've been in relationships with, what they thought was lacking, they will say they didn't get my time or attention. My void sucked it up. I was always running, reaching for the next thing, not valuing what I had, where I was or whom I was with. In my mind, I could always do better. I began to feel like the character of "Dexter" on the cable show. Not that I was a serial killer, but a person who could not feel. I expressed my feelings through having a good time with my friends, sex with the woman of the moment, but I couldn't feel anything.

The answer to the second has to do with my size. I was always a big boy and my brother often teased me about being fat. Well that coupled with my size made me self-conscious. I was always cautioned about being bigger than the other children so I was afraid to let loose, for fear of hurting someone. I never wanted that to happen which led to further repression. I've always envied the devil-may care people. The men in movies who were thought of a brash, rogues. That's my alter ego speaking from my void. It is the part of me that craves expression.

We seek partners to play the roles of those who denied us validation in the past. Our wife/husband plays the role of our aloof or disapproving mother/father. Our children become miniature versions of ourselves who we drive insane trying to correct all that didn't go well in our own childhood.

We put our children through the same situations that we experienced, when in fact they are new creations with their own purpose for being.

The next time you have difficulty with those closest to you, ask yourself what past role, from your life, are they playing. What scenario of denial are you re-enacting? My first marriage was difficult because I was re-enacting my relationship with my disapproving mother. While I was growing up, I tried everything to get her approval, to make her laugh, make her proud. One of the only things she ever commended me for was marrying the right woman. Perhaps that is because I married a miniature version of her. Are you putting up with a no-good man like your mother put up with your no-good father? Are you trying to win the love of the first love you lost?

You will be able to match your difficult relationships with ones that you experienced at a key point in your development. I call them **GHOST RELATIONSHIPS** because they are like spirits still waiting for a resolution. Like a ghost ship, cruising the ocean with a doomed crew waiting to be released from a curse.

That is why our relationships fail to evolve. Until we let go of our past, agree to no longer be that voided person, we cannot move to our next level of development. We are not free to love. We must not spend our lives reliving the past. In order to be free, we have to let it go.

nine

Goals: Got Some?

"Life become worthwhile when we have worthwhile goals."
— *Maxwell Maltz*

Every relationship that we will ever have is destined to fail unless we ask and answer the KEY LIFE QUESTION:

What is my Purpose? What have I been put here to do?

Your purpose is that thing that fills you up from the inside. It makes you happy to get out of bed in the morning and crazy about being who you are. You can't have a relationship with someone else until you have a relationship with yourself. This means knowing yourself and loving yourself. It means that you are happily utilizing your gifts to express your purpose for being on this planet. Your purpose is tied to your gift and we are all gifted.

If your mate is unaware of their purpose and you are oblivious to yours, then filling each other's voids is all that you can do. As we know, that satisfaction is temporary. Soon the dissatisfaction creeps back inside your mind. "There has to be more." Being bored and in search of what is better, people do things that appear totally out of character. I have done this myself, quite often. It is a self-rebellion of sorts that can have serious consequences.

I have seen men and women blindsided by affairs, shopping sprees, hijacked bank accounts and children out of wedlock, all because of undefined, unexpressed purpose. When a person doesn't know who they are or what they are here to do, they don't feel like a woman. It is like being blind. What do you think, a person in that position is going to do? They stumble around trying to find the good in life. Without a spiritual connection to self, they settle for what makes them feel good for the moment. The thing that satisfies their baser needs or is pleasing to their five senses.

I have been accused of trying to talk people out of being in relationships, giving excuses for men, including myself, for not moving forward with their unions, but what I'm telling you is without prejudice:

"Until a person is aware of and actively pursuing their life purpose, an evolving relationship is impossible."

Please take note of the word, evolving. Women have told me,

"Well he can find himself while he's married to me."

To that I say, "You're right, he can."

However, while he's finding his purpose, it may take him in a direction that is away from the life you desire as a couple. What then? Will you impede his development to satisfy your self? It is the same for men who try to get women to give up their dreams for the vision that he has for them. Contrary to popularized opinion, not every woman desires to be a wife and mother.

To make life great, we must become as children wild and free. Explore US in a loving manner. Give love without hesitation, without expectation of return. We must free ourselves of guilt for our actions and free ourselves of the burden of blaming others for love we don't have or didn't get. We must recognize that people act in line with how they think about themselves, specifically, what purpose they choose. What they do can only hurt if we expect something different from them. Many of us hold great resentment for parents who didn't show up to recitals, ball games and what have you. Or parents, who provided for baser needs, but weren't affectionate like on television. What we must realize is that if they didn't give it, maybe they didn't have it to give. Or maybe they did, but chose to give it to other children or another family or live a life devoted to them. We must forgive them and move on. In order to fill our own voids, we must let go of the hurt their behavior caused. Let it go.

If you don't know what your purpose is at this point, that's fine. It's time for a voyage of self-discovery. What do you DO, THINK or FEEL that can't be bought? Simply put, your purpose is inside of what you Love about YOU. It's what The Void can't suck up because it's available in an unlimited supply.

Once you have answered the question, look at your life and measure your past and present actions against your purpose. Do they align? If your dream is to become a rap star, I hope you aren't working as a mortician unless it's to pay for studio time. We must make sure that our goals and actions support each other or we could find ourselves getting in our own way.

We talk ourselves out of our dreams instead of nurturing them. Know that you have the power within to be all that you want and more, provided you truly want it. You must have a burning desire to see your dreams through no matter what other people say to the contrary.

You can do it. Believe, and then act.

ten

Get Your Life Back!

(Read this Chapter Daily)

"A wave of faith leads to an ocean of hope."
— *D.W. Leonard*

Picture a high-powered engine pounding away, day after day in service of its chassis (body). Its job is to perform at peak efficiency. Then a seal ruptures, the engine loses its drive. Its power drops off placing stress on the other parts until the engine blows. The car stops.

The powerful engine is YOU. You are a miracle of design. Banging at peak efficiency until Voids form. Suddenly, your power drops you become listless, cranky, dissatisfied. Everything becomes a chore. You complain incessantly, feel stressed all the time until your whole body goes. You feel unable to move from your current position or situation. Healing and sealing your voids will give you back your power. Use these **FIVE VOID HEALERS** to change your Life:

1) <u>LET GO!</u>

Let go of EVERYTHING. The things we hold onto keep us feeling stuck. We hold onto unfaithful spouses, friends that hate us, money issues that weigh us down and people that don't inspire us. The incorrect belief is that these things are holding us, when in fact, we are holding onto them. The payoff for being stuck is familiarity. Our issue with letting go and moving on is that we don't know what will happen when we leave our comfort zone. We believe that moving on, letting go of what we know, is scary. But if our comfort zone is so comfortable, why don't we feel good?

If you need to tell the boss to kiss your ass and leave a dead end job, do it. If you need a divorce, get it. If you need to rebuild a relationship, do it. If you need to start or stop talking to someone to be at peace, do it now. Stop using words like "process" or "timing" to hide your fear of moving on. Heal that Void. Let it all go. Say to yourself: Whatever happens, whoever becomes unhappy as a result of my choices - I CAN HANDLE IT. I will not die. But picture yourself in the same place 2, 4, 6 years from now. Now THAT is scary.

DAILY MANTRA: WHATEVER HAPPENS, I CAN HANDLE IT.

2) <u>VALUE UP</u>:

Recognize Your Value to You. My Aunt Judith killed herself everyday to make sure everyone had what they needed. She made sure her husband had lunch, the kids got to every practice and social event in the world. My aunt made sure the home was clean and ready to welcome guests twenty-four hours a day. Most of all, she fed anyone who would stop by. Now she did this out of love and I love her for it, but she wore herself out.

Where was the help? Where was her chance to explore and feel good about herself? Maybe working for everyone filled her up. If that fills you up, that's wonderful. But if you are drained, stressed and wondering where your life went, you need to Value Up. Put yourself first for a little while to regain balance. Some won't do it because they feel that it is selfish. I do not believe that putting your needs first is selfish, but necessary. It's like that spiel they give you during the safety drill on the airplane. If you don't place the oxygen mask over your own face first, you may not be able to help anyone else. If you are gone, what good are you?

Time for you is good. It's necessary in order to keep yourself going. It's natural. Embrace it. Stop feeling guilty. I think it's just as bad to be self-less. In order to have a productive life, you need balance. Some time for me, then some time for others, in that order. LIVE with harmony at your center and life will serve you in serving others. Heal that Void.

DAILY MANTRA - TIME FOR ME IS GOOD.

3) <u>BUILD YOUR BODY TEMPLE!</u>

Your body is a sacred place. Get into the best physical and spiritual shape of your life, starting today. The key to success is simple. Let the positive thoughts about your body drive your mind to action. Do not let working out become a chore, but rather a labor of love. Hold your expanding areas (rolls) every morning; tell them that you love them. Hold your entire body in your embrace and tell it that you love it.

Don't make jokes to your friends about being overweight or eating too much. Your body has ears and will react to what it hears. Its feelings can be hurt. Then it will seek food as solace, which is not the direction you want to travel. You don't have to join a gym or push iron, but you have to get moving.

Whatever you love to do, do it.

My old coach use to tell me to, "Walk, jog, hike, row, swim or ride a bike." Your mind and body are one. You can't free one while the other is captive. Let go of that image of you being the Rock. Just maintain a healthy, toned body, for whatever your type. Meditate, do yoga, do something. The important part is that you dedicate positive energy to the place in which you will spend the rest of your life. You only get one, so appreciate it. Show it.

DAILY MANTRA: I LOVE MY BODY; I LOVE MY MIND.

4) RIDE THE HORSE!

Say "Yes" to Life. This is my absolute favorite. Ride the Horse means to indulge all of your dreams, whims and fantasies. What you want is not bad or wrong. Refuse to feel guilty or sad about past or present choices. Live only in this one perfect moment. As long as our intent is to live life to the fullest and share with others, we are not wrong. So don't break any laws or violate anyone else's person. Get out there and live. Do all the things you haven't done in years. Go to carnival, swim with the dolphins. Call that childhood friend you haven't spoken with in years.

Forgive those whose actions caused you to give yourself pain and move on. I know women who are afraid to go to the movies because they are taking time away from the family. Go see that movie even if your girlfriends can't make it. Make yourself happy. Buy something nice for you, just because. Party like a rock star. We have been given one precious life. What are you waiting for?

DAILY MANTRA: I MAKE MYSELF HAPPY EVERYDAY!

5) CELEBRATE YOU!

Wake up every morning, clap your hands together and give thanks for the person you are, for your specific manifestation of the creator. Recognize that you haven't lost any of your time in life. If you haven't had the chance to fulfill your wildest dreams, do it today. If you feel your life is not going anywhere or you've suffered from poor health, it's MORE important that you celebrate.

Close your eyes. See yourself as a whole, perfect, creation then act as if. Act as if this life is a wonderful journey because it truly is just that. When you let your precious life give birth to something new, each day, everyday becomes your birthday.

DAILY MANTRA: EVERYDAY IS MY BIRTHDAY!

You're not stuck, your thinking is!

The wonderful part about filling your voids is that you finally realize what has been keeping you stuck all these years. Why you have never felt man enough, pretty enough or like a good enough parent? You are more than worthy of the life you seek if you give yourself the permission to let go of the thoughts that tie you down. Thoughts that keep you from experiencing the awesome power that is yours from birth.

But we must not fall into the trap. In the business world we call it "Admiring the data." That means you have all of the information, but take no action. In order to live the life you desire, you have to MOVE. You have to do something different then you have done before. Don't sit there thinking, "So that's why I do that," for the next ten years with the power to change resting in your mind. Your life is in your hands.

Part of the road to change is practicing Hardcore Love of yourself and others. Come back and read this chapter as long as it takes to build self-confidence toward healing those Voids.

You can do it. Live the life you want, today.

eleven

Hardcore Love
Your Best Relationship!

"Never love anyone who treats you like you're ordinary."
— *Oscar Wilde*

You've healed all of your voids and you are ready to Love. How do you do it right? The concept of Hardcore Love was formed out of the frustration of non-evolving relationships. If you are like me, you often find yourself in pain wondering why things didn't work out. "Why am I so unlucky at Love?" The truth is, "luck" has nothing to do with it. And you didn't fail at Love. You reached a level, which I like to call a Development Point or DEV POINT and got stuck there. Your love never evolved. I like to call it, Elevated Love. Science teaches us that water is necessary for life, but stagnant water is death because of the bacteria that builds up in it. The same is true of all relationships. A relationship that doesn't move is dead.

Through the Hardcore Philosophy, you will be able to identify your relationships Dev Point and truthfully assess whether elevation is possible. Non-Elevating Relationships are often problematic. They get in the way of the couple developing a relationship based on equality. An equality-based relationship is one that has the power to become a union, meaning the couple think and act as ONE. But before we get to that point, the first question we all must answer is, "Are you happy?"

Understand that Hardcore Love means loving a person with your complete mind, body and spirit. It requires that you hold NOTHING back. Experts have told us over the years that you should hold back in love. They suggest that you love an individual from a comfort zone. You will hear me refer to these couples as Eighty-Fivers. They represent eighty-five percent of all relationships. People in commitments they neither respect nor obey. They stagnate and never achieve a true state of unconditional love. The other five percent of relationships are free, filled with acceptance and mutual discovery.

Some people maintain Face book Relationships. They settle for "Like." Like is a four-letter word that corrupts all it touches. Love the hell out of someone or leave them alone. You like chewing gum, but you don't want a relationship with it. We are finite beings with no time to waste. "Like" is a crime because it steals your most precious asset, time.

THE LOVE LESSON:

Hardcore Love teaches us to work towards Love in a state of total abandon, in which we hold nothing in reserve. It means we think of our needs as well as those of our partner. Neither takes a back seat. We listen and respect our partners without feeling depreciated. We reveal our true selves to each other through honest communication, unafraid of loss. We make love with complete abandon, not fearing social morays. It is the love the Creator gave us at our birth. It's the love your soul has yearned for your entire life. HARDCORE.

No, I am not freaking crazy. This is not the love you give to everyone. It is Love Elevated to its highest form. A love seldom seen, but chances are you've glimpsed it. That couple that stares at each other with adoring eyes, hangs on each other's words during dinner then plays grab ass on the way to the car. You know what's going to happen when they get home. Something straight out of "Fifty Shades of Grey." Meanwhile in your relationship, you barely look at each other during the meal, walk in silence to the car and you know what's going to happen when you get home. Nothing. You'll peck kiss and fall asleep to Arsenio.

You are in a "Like" Relationship while LOVE is elevating all around you. In the middle of my "Like" Relationship, I can remember going to Dunkin' Donuts one morning. On my way out of the store, I landed behind a couple clearly in lust. Granted, it could have been the Oxygen Phase, but they looked like they had been together for some time. They were middle aged, hugging and kissing. Then she encircled his waist with her arm, placed her hand in his pocket, and playfully squeezed his butt. Suddenly, I was overcome with such jealousy I wanted to run and kick them in the back. Where was my passion? Where was my fire? I had settled, become still like the water. My relationship was dead. Do not accept a Zombie Relationship with yourself or with others. Hardcore Love is the highest truth. Trust and believe that you deserve love at its best.

It is the way you can make the Oxygen Phase last forever. Each day you look at your relationship with new eyes. So open your mind a little further and get the best relationship you have ever had. Accept nothing less. You deserve Love at its best.

twelve

Hardcore Love
Spelled Out

8 STAGES OF RELATIONSHIP DEVELOPMENT - (DEV POINTS)

1. HONESTY
2. ATTRACTION
3. REVELATION
4. DESIRE
5. COMMITMENT
6. OBEDIENCE
7. RESPECT
8. EQUALITY

HONESTY - THE FOUNDATION

It is the pull from our voids that gives us the feeling of attraction and not love. It gives us that feeling of kinship. That feeling that there is a connection, because there is, and it's very deep. We attract people who will fill our voids. People who will bring us face to face with our true self.

The ironic part of the Honesty Stage is that most of us tell lies. This "Getting to know you" time could set the foundation for an amazing relationship, if we told the truth. Instead we put our best foot forward hoping the target of our affection will believe that we are flawless. Nine times out of ten, the warts are visible. Our true imperfect selves can be glimpsed if one looks closely enough. They do not. Our prospect is too busy hiding their imperfections. Like roaches on an apartment wall when company visits, we act as if they aren't there. The power of infatuation causes us to submit to our fantasy of the person instead of the truth right before our eyes.

We don't have to be blunt or crass about it, but we should be firm about our standards for operation. As one friend once told me, "My love is unconditional, but my relationships aren't." If you want us to interact, you will treat me in this fashion. This is how we will relate. This is how we will walk together.

Before you leap into the next stage of developing your relationship, you need to know if there are any DEAL BREAKERS. Situations that give you pause about proceeding with this person. For those of you shy about asking, here is a handy checklist.

DO YOU HAVE ANY PAST OR CURRENT:

MARRIAGES - Funny how they tend to pop up later.

CHILDREN - They pop up too. How many? How much time do you spend with them?

MENTAL HEALTH ISSUES - Are you Bi-Polar? Diabetic? Impotent?

DRUG DEPENDENCE - If they take Tylenol regularly, you need to know.

FINANCES - Credit card debt, alimony, child support? How much?

CRAZY EX-GIRL/BOYFRIENDS - Baby mama/daddy drama.

This is not being "nosy" and you are not trying to scare the person away, however, we cannot agree or plan for situations of which we are unaware. To be blunt, you should know what you're getting into, beforehand. Once you are emotionally attached, you will agree to anything just to "make it work." Don't get blindsided by what was there all the time. It is better to offend than have to defend. And if you are considering marriage, understand, what's theirs becomes yours and this includes debts and obligations.

BE HONEST WITH YOURSELF!

In order to start a journey through life with someone, we must know our current position and where we want to go. If someone else is going with us, we need to know where they are going and if traveling together is beneficial. Maybe I don't want to travel with someone who is going to a destination too far out of my way. You get the point? I know. I take all the romance out of it. The mystery. A mystery doesn't stay a mystery for long, so you are better off knowing sooner than later. In order to start thinking about a relationship with someone, you should ask these questions.

3 LIFE PLAN QUESTIONS:

1) WHAT IS MY LIFE PURPOSE? (Why am I here?)
2) WHAT IS THEIR LIFE PURPOSE? (Do they know?)
3) WHAT CAN WE BUILD TOGETHER? (Do we have a common mission?)

MY PURPOSE?

Why are you here? What have you been put on this planet to do? I hear some of you saying, "That's a hard question." You doggone right it is. It's a question that determines how you spend the rest of your time on this planet.

Think. A book has a topic. It follows that topic from beginning to the middle through to the end. When we finish reading it we can talk about its message or what it meant to us.

People are the same way. There is a message inside all of us. Something unique we were put here to share with the world. People that wander around without purpose are called transients. Why would we ever consider being transient in something as important as our life?

I hear some of you saying, "Well, we can figure it out together while we are on the journey." Is that the best way to go? If you were leaving home, to travel to an unfamiliar place, would you just get in a car and go? Forget maps or a GPS, just drive around until you find it? You could do it, but think of all the time you'll spend in frustration asking others where to go, getting mad with each other for not knowing the way. Doesn't that sound like some relationships you know?

YOU CAN'T GIVE SOMEONE YOUR PURPOSE.

Some of you set out on rescue missions. You find a transient or someone unaware of their purpose and decide to give them yours. Your going someplace, why shouldn't they tag along? They love having a place to go even if it isn't their own. Then somewhere along the way they start expressing strong dissatisfaction, with YOU. They are adamant about having their own dreams, bigger than yours, and they will no longer be your side-kick. You shake your head at the betrayal, the utter ingratitude.

You cannot give another person your purpose. If you are a religious or spiritual leader you may assist them in finding their own path, but who wants to do that in a relationship? Your mate sees you as a peer and will take your guidance as you trying to control them. I have seen this type of rebellion break up many romantic unions as well as friendships.

WHAT IS A POWER COUPLE?

In order for two people to have a future together they must be on purpose, their goals coinciding in a way that neither feels lessened. They must both have a burning desire to reach them allowing neither internal stress or external setbacks halt their progress. When the Bible speaks of a couple being "Equally yoked," I believe this to be the meaning. For those who can merge purpose and be on fire about its success, it is an awesome spectacle. This is the true meaning of "Power Couple."

thirteen

Attraction

"*Wise people do not fall in Love. They walk in.*"
— *D.W. Leonard*

The Attraction Stage, of Hardcore Love, is also the Oxygen Stage. A stage where you allow the person be he or her self. A time before demands are placed upon one another. You feel the attraction without the draining affect of your voids, because they are only activated by your expectations. This is a wonderful time when your only need is for the other person to be in your presence.

Your mate and you talk on the phone for hours at a time. You exchange slow kisses that are the best you've ever had. Hold hands in public and think about each other when you're apart. The person becomes the air you breathe, like Oxygen. You truly feel as if you will die without them. You are completely vulnerable, willing to give your entire being to this union. It is at this point we should ask a crucial question. What exactly am I attracted to?

WHAT IS ATTRACTING ME?

Think about the driving force behind your attraction. Does it come from a place of abundance, of sincerely wanting to share an already rich life? Or does it come from a place rooted in want or need, which is another name for fear? If you both are not whole and on purpose, the desire you feel is rooted in fear. The attraction is your void demanding to be filled. What you seek is directly in line with what you feel is lacking in your own life. It is an attempt to replay the critical point, in your development, which created your void. Physical maturity does not free us from our voids. Being aware of them and changing the thinking that feeds the behavior, does.

Many of us have heard the saying, "Opposites attract." Yes and no. Opposites that complement each other do attract, but the greater attraction is to that which will make us feel confident where we are fearful. You hear it all the time. A woman, who believes that she is no good with math, will marry an accountant.

All of our fears are rooted in our voids. Many women have expressed to me that they need someone to help them in life. They are frustrated with having to do it all themselves. Deep down, they fear being alone or being the social outcast. All of their couple friends ask them the same question at every function they attend. "So, when are you going to get married?" If they are already married, "When are you going to have children? Don't you want babies?" For many women and men the question is a dagger through the heart each time it is asked.

The implied thought is that they are not good enough to have a man or woman want them on a permanent basis. That they are somehow UNWORTHY of Love. Being in a relationship no more indicates a person is desirable than being in a car means they can drive. In both cases, it is the ability to get where you are going that is important. And that has nothing to do with whoever wants, likes or loves us.

If you do not enjoy your own company to the fullest, you are not ready for a relationship. As stated in the previous chapter, you can't hide from your voids in someone else's. It will feel good, but the affect is temporary. It is imperative that we love being with ourselves first, last and always. No matter who comes and goes in our lives, we must remain in love with ourselves. We must enjoy being with ourselves so much that we want to share that abundance with some-one else. In order to do that, we must seal and heal our voids. Love made of peace is strong and elevating. Love made of need is weak and draining.

Don't get me wrong, a relationship of need can be carried on, but it will not elevate to equality, which is the goal of all meaningful unions. We attract who we are. Think about yourself right now. Take a good look at your insecurities, fears, bad habits and all. Be honest. Would you want to be in a long-term relationship with that person? Would their/your outlook on life inspire you? Just because a person desires you, as is, doesn't mean that's the best way for you to live. Seal your voids first.

AFFIRMATION: I ATTRACT WHO I AM.

fourteen

Revelation

"In order to please others, we lose our hold on our life's purpose."
— *Epictetus*

No matter who we pretend to be, the Revelation Stage is where the true person shows up. This is where the rubber meets the road. Let's say I'm not a party animal. I'm more like a couch potato, but I pretend to be outgoing to win the interest of a woman. At Revelation, I start making excuses or outright lying in order to stay in the house. Why? Shouldn't my potential mate know and love me for who I am? Yes. But how many of us are brave enough to share who we truly are. We show them what they want to see, out of the fear of scaring them away, which is the problem.

Revelation should be time that happy dialogue takes place as to the possible function of being together, long-term. Again, this should take place in a pressure free environment. It doesn't have to be heavy and you don't have to ambush each other with toxic phrases such as, "Can I talk to you?" Rather it should be the time when we lay it on the table. This is who I am and this is what I want. These are my deal breakers; this is what I'm flexible about. Game players will use this time to tell lies, understand, that what a person reveals must be backed up by desire and action.

If a woman tells me she wants to be a doctor, I want to see her tuition payment for medical school. If a man tells you he wants to be a writer, ask to see his current manuscript. If it's a dream without action, so is the person. You are not going to take him/her anywhere they don't want to go.

Most relationships suffer misunderstanding in the area of sex. Intimacy is not often a topic of discussion, especially where marriage is concerned. We just take for granted that it occurs. When our mate says, "I love sex," our response is often, "Yeah, me too." Not all of us do, but we pretend because we don't want to lose the person. I've known women who have engaged in frequent sex with their spouses/boyfriends for years without pleasure. They don't hate sex, but they don't love it. It's not a priority to them. Why didn't this come out during the early stages of the relationship? Fear.

The problem is, our mates will not remain ignorant for long. What we don't like will manifest itself, then what? Affairs and drama that is completely unnecessary. These can be avoided if we would just reveal our true selves. There is someone in the world for everyone, who truly wants someone. No one needs hide who they are, or what they need, for fear of being alone. We need to fear a compromise that erodes our souls day by day.

Muted desire turns into a poison that can destroy the quality of your life, regardless of your financial status. The "quiet desperation" written about by Thoreau in which we feel as if what we long to be or do will burst from our chest. "The truth shall make you free," is a great saying. This freedom comes from the truth of accepting yourself. Love demands that we embrace, not hide ourselves.

Accepting our own truth is the highest form of Love. When we reveal that truth to another it is symbolic of the revelation and acceptance that must take place within self. In fact, it's a mutual understanding, which is the foundation of Love. When we put forth a false face to someone else it is an external rejection of your internal self. This self-rejection, I believe, is at the root of all our suffering. It disconnects us from the source of all abundant love. Our spirit. That stuff inside us that tells us how we feel about ourselves. Tells us that we are connected to something greater. Tells us that the world is a good place filled with Love.

So let us make the agreement that we will hide our truth from no one for the sake of acceptance or what this world deems as love. Note: I use the lower case L in the case of any mention of this world's love as opposed with the true Love that we find within self. A Love bestowed on us at the time of our birth, to be shared with all those we meet in this life. People may choose to Love us or not, but we must focus on loving the truth within ourselves.

MANTRA: I LOVE MYSELF AND SHARE THAT LOVE WITH OTHERS.

fifteen
Desire

IS SEX, EVIL?

"Few things in life are better than the person you are in love with desiring your mind as much as your body."
— D.W. Leonard

Is my desire wrong? Is what I want evil? I don't believe that any of us come from an evil place. Some of you are shaking your heads now, but let us reason. If we all come from the same energy, wherever you believe it resides, how can some of us be better than others? Our emanation is the same. What we refer to as good or evil is the result brought about by our focus. We often evaluate these results as positive or negative when, in truth, they are only results.

For instance, sex is positive and life giving. To focus on sex alone without the influence of understanding, of communication, of purpose, robs it of its power. The pursuit of sex, absent of Love, brings about misunderstanding with others, then suffering.

If this is not our intended result then we need to adjust our focus. To label our actions negative or bad is to throw garbage down the well from which we intend to drink. I believe the same in the realm of our desires. Wanting is not wrong. However, focusing on an object alone such as money or power can corrupt its energy. Corrupt meaning; rob of its intended purpose. As in all things, the "want" needs a "why." What you want, and why you want it, will lead you to your purpose. Results are evaluated according to how close or how far your decisions take you in relation to your Life Purpose. Are your results in line with your purpose or driving your further away.

One of the definitions of the word negative is "being without rewards, results or effectiveness." There is nothing that we do that fits that category. The result is the reward. Like a slot machine, some hit big, some just hit. But there's always a result. We must stop beating ourselves up emotionally when situations do not go the way we desire. For our disappointment is the result of our expectations, not the result of our actions. Our actions, aligned with our purpose, always yield results in the correct direction. There is no wasted time as long as there is purposeful motion. Believing you failed to achieve your purpose because of one or two or two million undesired results is a product of your fear. Every result means something. Every result is a reward for your effort. Many times our emotional disappointment obscures the benefit we received. We are so busy feeling the shame of "losing" we do not realize that we won, something.

After we have revealed ourselves in a relationship, we WANT the object of our desire to be ours. Why?

If we haven't completely sealed our voids, the WHY is suspect. **This is why many marriages fail.** Fail meaning to not achieve their intended purpose. Our relationships have enough desire to get us to the point of Desire, but not enough to get us to our highest point, which is equality. Let me make it plain:

1. **We want the person. (Desire)**
2. **We get them in our lives. (Fulfillment)**
3. **We have no idea what to do with them. (Confusion)**

Then, creeping boredom or dissatisfaction comes knocking.

THINK. Without an understanding of our true need, we are left with our inner detective trying to solve the mystery of the person.

7 RELATIONSHIP MYSTERIES:

1. WHAT ARE THEY LIKE AT HOME/WORK/PLAY?
2. WHAT ARE THEY LIKE WHEN THEY GO OUT?
3. WHAT ARE THEY LIKE WHEN THEY ARE NAKED?
4. WHAT ARE THEY LIKE AROUND THEIR FAMILY?
5. WHAT ARE THEY LIKE AROUND CHILDREN?
6. WHAT ARE THEY LIKE UNDER PRESSURE/SICK?
7. WHAT ARE THEY LIKE IN BED? (Kinky?)

Face it! Once these mysteries are solved, the spell is broken. We are left with a person who farts in their sleep and hogs the covers. All of the chemistry goes right out the window, unless we are guided by our purpose. Ten or fifteen years into a relationship, you find yourself thinking, there has to be something more. Is this all that there is to life: A job that doesn't inspire me, watching my kids grow up and tolerating my mate?

We start searching for diversions via PEA (People, Events & Activities) that we target to fill this Void. We seek something to rekindle our desire. It's a cycle that repeats itself like the rising and setting of the sun. People searching for a new mystery to be solved when, in truth, they haven't begun to explore the greatest mystery in the world: SELF!

Our desire should be self-directed. We should first want to know all there is to know about US. Joining with someone else on this journey is a way to gather more information about you. You might also start a journey together to assist each other, however, the US cannot take the place of exploring and loving yourself. So embrace your desire. Fall in love with the mystery that yearns to be solved every day that you open your eyes. What can I give back to the creator for the awesome gift of my life?

This is the starting point of all elevating unions. The desire to know self is the fire that burns inside every one of us. There is always more to learn until the light fades from us and takes hold in another being who will again desire to know self, to Love. Learning, then acting in accord with your Life Purpose is a life well lived.

This is why it is crucial that you and your mate are working on your purpose. And if you choose a relationship, your purpose must align and feed each other. Working together, sharing with each other keeps things brand new. You will take on adventures everyday. Inspire each other to new heights. We are attracted, by the mystery of a person, like detectives. However, a mystery doesn't stay that way for long.

The creator has given us the ability to focus our Love, our thoughts and our energy. It's called "Choice." Choose to focus on YOU. Let the power flow through you without any thought of trapping it. Me is truth; mine is illusion. For everything that you desire is already yours. It is inside the love you have for yourself. Share it.

MANTRA: TO KNOW MYSELF IS TO KNOW OTHERS.

sixteen

Commitment

"Freedom is not the absence of commitments, but the ability to choose - and commit myself to - what is best for me."
-Paulo Coelho

When I give talks about relationships, invariably an audience member will state that they would like a mate who is "committed." I usually respond by telling them that ALL of their past and future mates are committed. The question is, "To Whom?"

If I asked you to commit your life to a total stranger, you would think that I was insane. This is because, in our experience, people are usually committed to people they know or to those with whom they have established a relationship. I believe people commit to what they have thought about or dreamt about every day of their lives since they were children. Why we believe their commitment will encompass how WE believe they should behave baffles me. We mistakenly think that, because we Love someone, they will do what we say.

That they will behave in a manner that reflects our desires.

Anyone who has been a child under parental supervision, or been the parental overseer, knows this not to be the case. This is especially true around the teenage years. Defiance seems to go hand in hand with the activation of hormones. Try as we might, they do as they will. The same should be thought of about our relationships.

A wise person once said, "Your expectations pave the way to your disappointments." The truth is, people will act in accord with the dream of their life. How they always hoped it would unfold. We will stumble, often blindly, after the taste of the sweet nectar of life, whatever we deem it to be. We cannot hope to bridle that horse, for it is during the running that it will discover itself, in truth. This discovery cannot occur while it is in the stable. If you Love your mate, let them go. Allow them to be who they are in every facet of their life. Make no demands on them, for what they wish to give, they will provide without request. If their freedom does not harmonize with what you desire in a relationship, then part. When we ask those, whom we love, to subvert their spirit for our comfort, we create a situation that cannot endure. One day, their true nature will emerge.

Within a romantic relationship we can only give understanding to action. Understanding is Love. So when a person, to whom we have given our Love, does something that speaks of NOT being committed to us, that is in fact the case. I expect my mate to be committed to her self, with every thought, word and deed. I am never disappointed.

Well maybe a little, but the burden is mine, not hers. This is why discovering what the person believes to be their Life Purpose or Life Dream is critical before beginning a relationship. It gives you a blueprint of their commitment. Read it. If a woman tells me that she will do anything to be an actress/model, I should not place designs on her as a housewife.

My friends tell me horror stories about women/men who have "cheated" on them. I tell them that it's not possible to cheat on another person in a relationship.

I had friends who were newly married to other mates, but they had a chemistry that filled the room. They tried to suppress it, play the best buds, brother and sister role. Eventually it became unbearable. They had to make a choice. They could live a lie and remain with their betrothed or face the truth. They loved each other from the moment they met and there wasn't a darn thing they could do about it. Their commitment is to be happy. To live lives that speak of power and joy with the precious time the creator has allotted. Therefore, it is impossible to "cheat" or be unfaithful to another person because you owe fidelity to yourself and your creator, only.

During meetings, I have watched people get up in arms about that statement. I know it sounds harsh. It is not our job to make others happy. They have themselves. You can tell a person something that is not the truth or lie to them. And if you make an agreement, via marriage, you should abide by it. However, you are allowed to change your mind, inform your partner and change your life to whatever you desire, without being unfaithful.

You are being faithful to the most important person in your life, YOU. This act does not make you bad. Get your life, because you cannot live someone else's. I know it is difficult to go against the roar of the crowd. To commit to what we know. It must be done if we are to elevate our relationships. Elevate our lives. No lies can exist within us or they will exist within everything we touch. So if your family tells you to make due, play it safe, go along with the program, don't do it. Cause one day it will all blow up. Better you make peace with yourself than live an unworthy life. An unworthy life is one in which you lie to others, in order to keep from hurting their feelings, and in doing so, you hurt their feelings and your own. You lie to yourself.

Again, if you take on the mantle of commitment, within the confines of a relationship agreement, respect it. Do not put yourself in positions that call upon you to repress your true self. We seek joy in the night only to hide it with the rising of the sun. Some mistakenly believe that they can create a jigsaw life. Pieces of pleasure are strung together in pursuit of happiness.

Why play those games when you could be living the full, honest Life you've always wanted? Why grind along on the donkey when the ride of your brilliant steed waits. Overkill, but you get the point. Why remain silent when you have a voice that could heal humanity. Let your music out. Strengthen your commitment to YOU and all of your commitments will be stronger.

MANTRA: I AM FULLY COMMITTED TO MYSELF.

seventeen

Obedience

"As the twig is bent, so grows the tree."
- *Old Proverb*

What will happen if we don't OBEY?

All our lives we are taught to obey. As babies we are taught to heed our parents, as students we are commanded to obey teachers and as adults we must obey the law. So much for free will. What if I do not obey? What will happen? It is in this area our greatest voids are formed. Voids rooted in fear of authority.

The penalty for disobedience has always been the threat of some kind of loss. If we don't obey teachers, we lose recess. If we don't obey the law, we lose our freedom. These are terrifying prospects, but none worse than that of not obeying our parents. The threat there, though never stated, is a loss of love. This threat forms Grand Canyon like Voids in our minds. The disapproval of our parents looms large. How could we ever dare disobey those that love us?

In my travels, I have found that love is not only a tie that binds, but also a chain that enslaves, if misused. The paradox, I have found, is that we must often disobey those we Love, in order to obey them. The ones that love us tell us that they desire our happiness. That happiness can only exist within a person free from undermining Voids. In order to make our happiness, we must listen to that all-important inner voice. The voice that tells us when we are feeling in spirit. The voice that would show us the path to our eternal happiness, if we would only heed it.

To listen to our inner voice, over the voice of the people that we love, is to invite the withdrawal of real and imagined benefits, including love. A love rooted in condition. It says that, if you do what I say, good things will happen. If you do not obey me, there will be a life-altering catastrophe. This is ridiculous, but accepted by many of us as factual. Our voids make it real. They say that we cannot live happily without our current money, jobs, and homes. That we should hold onto relationships and spouses, that don't inspire us, because we may not be able to find anything better. FEAR. What if no one else wants you? To those that love us, our staying in position, changing nothing from year to year, pleases them. We appear stable. Unwittingly, we allow this fear of movement to cut us off from our true happiness. It keeps us from learning more about our self.

For our first steps, we are given a hug and kiss. Our graduation from school brings us gifts and even a new car. Getting married brings gifts, the well wishes of family and the validation of society. You become a solid citizen. All these things seem wonderful. They reinforce our obedience to the status quo. All is well, until we want to try something else. To go against what has been established as the "good" in life: stability.

When we decide to change, to disobey, we often hear, "You can't do that." "A smart/good/responsible/sane person doesn't do that." The same people, events and activities that rewarded your progress, suddenly question your reason. You and I have heard of people who have given up six figure salaries to travel the world in order to find themselves. You have heard about athletes who choose academic scholarships over tickets to the big leagues. Comedians who give up 50 million dollar TV shows and flee the country.

We say, "He's crazy. If I had all that money, I would do..." Therein lies the problem. How much is your happiness worth? Would you take 3 million dollars a year to be a slave? To not be able to exercise your creativity and free will? What if I'm supposed to play a game and I just feel like walking on the beach? What if I'm under contract to hit or be hit by someone and I no longer desire to be violent? Lots of money sounds good, at the outset. What if, after few months, you want to do something else? Then what? There is no amount of money can silence the music of your heart. The music that sings of your divine purpose in this world. It reminds you of your greatest good.

Break the chains. Listen to your heart, your voice, and your spirit: Let it go, Ride the horse and take a chance. Be the shining star you were intended to be at your conception. There is no such thing as "can't." It doesn't exist. There is nothing in this world that you cannot do. Ignore external voices; listen to the voice from within. No matter how much you love your family or friends, being miserable to gain their approval is too high a price to pay. Taking chances can be scary. You don't know what's going to happen. Neither do I. I can't even promise you a "happy" ending or a result that you will like better than the one you anticipated. What I can promise you is growth. No regrets. No, "what ifs."

You will have a result that will change you forever. And that's an awesome thing. You will never be the same. Isn't that what life is all about? It's not gambling if you bet on yourself. It's faith. I know you believe in yourself. If you didn't, this book wouldn't be in your hand. You have it because you've been searching for something, a way to change. You are ready.

You have found it. It's inside you. I am with you, I believe in you. Only you have the power to change your life. Do it while you have the time. If your inner voice is urging you to take a chance, to change. Listen. It doesn't have to be perfect. It has to come from the heart. Take a chance on YOU. You know what is right for you. Trust it. Take a step toward freedom today.

MANTRA: I OBEY MY INNER VOICE. IT CALLS ME TOWARD MY HIGHEST GOOD.

eighteen
Respect

Is your Respect, disrespectful?

Respect for others is a much-debated topic. People often tell us whom we should respect and to what degree. Celebrities or "stars" should be shown the utmost respect due to their accomplishments and social position. Elders should be respected for their time and wisdom. Children should be respected for their youth. People of alternate lifestyles should be respected for their difference. Amid all the hoopla about respect, no one has taken the time to define it.

Respect, in my humble opinion, is favor or partiality. We are partial to whom or what we love. The problem arises when this favor causes us to place the talents, abilities or uniqueness of others above our own. Not only do we subjugate ourselves in the bright light of celebrities, but also we do it in our personal relationships. Is this type of respect, disrespectful?

A friend of mine has never been star struck. She has always viewed celebrities as ordinary people, with the exception of Michael Jackson. This concept of respect was shared with her during her youth, by her parents. She was taught to view everyone as valuable with none being superior because of wealth or station. I found this virtue remarkable and decided to take it as one of my own. I now believe that I should favor or be partial to all beings, young, and old, rich, impoverished because we are all made of the same stuff. We are all mostly water with minerals added so why be nervous around people just like you? We are all stars, unique, divine. I transferred that same view to my view of relationships.

Our voids contribute to our maintaining a low opinion of ourselves. The result is we laude other people while neglecting self. As a teacher of middle school students, I would test student self esteem by asking a question. "Who is the most attractive person in the room?" No hands would go up. Some may have believed it privately, but didn't want to hold themselves above their mates. I would follow by telling them that beauty is in the eye of the person beholding it. I cannot tell you what standard you should respect. Everyone favors something different. It is the same way with respect.

The people or things you respect were formed from your voids during childhood. Whatever you considered greater than yourself, you adopted as your respect standard. You held up what you didn't have. You put on a pedestal what you wanted or thought you should want to attain because your pillars told you it was good. Your respect did not form naturally, but out of a controlled manipulation.

It's time to seal that Void.

<u>You owe respect to yourself, first and foremost.</u> Be partial and favor yourself above all else. See yourself in the light in which you were created. Then, and this is the biggest part, share that light, life and love with the rest of the world. It doesn't work any other way. It is impossible to value others without first valuing yourself. Respect, not born of self, is destructive. Groupies, idol worshipers, fanatics are people who value the lives and talents of others above their own. Our life energy is much greater than that.

Ask yourself a key question. Who do you see yourself as less than? Are you as great as those you admire? Are the seeds of greatness dormant within you while you are a fan of another person's gift? Do not cheat yourself, or the world, by being an eternal fan. Let someone's expression of his or her talents inspire you to explore your own, more deeply. To truly be in harmony in our relationships, we must feed our spirits till they burst with Love for our own being. Then let it pour out without measure. Love for self, love for others flows from the same place, beloved.

Do you still doubt? Think about your own respected moments, things and people. Do you love them for what they mean to you or for what others say they should mean? Understanding why we respect people or things is a key to healing and sealing the Void in our self-worth. Understanding ourselves is the key to our freedom. They show us the door, but we still must open it and walk through.

I have known men and women who wonder why they are treated poorly in relationships. It is the way they perceive self and the treatment they believe they deserve. When my friends and I were in high school, we could spot girls with low self-esteem just by watching the way they moved through the hallway, their posture, the way they carried their books. We knew these girls were easy prey for physical contact, because they didn't believe in their worth. Many of them were beautiful girls that only needed encouragement and some style to shine, but they didn't believe it, so it didn't manifest. Self-image + Self-esteem = Self Worth. If you don't recognize your gifts, you won't value yourself. See yourself as a product of the divine.

Respect yourself.

MANTRA: MY RESPECT FOR OTHERS FLOWS FROM SELF LOVE.

nineteen

Equality

The Highest Point!

The eighth is the highest level to which a relationship can ascend. This is called an **ELEVATED UNION**. These unions are only possible after both partners have healed their voids and working on their life purpose. You will know you have attained elevation when three components are present and active between your partner and yourself.

1. <u>I know what I want!</u>
2. <u>I've created a Plan.</u>
3. <u>I'm working my Plan.</u>

What is needed is a PLAN for when, why, and how you are to be together. And in order to form an US plan, we must first have a ME plan. I know I've stated it several times, but it's that simple. Many of us have a general idea of what we want to do in life, but nothing concrete and we feel very little pressure to come up with something.

We look at friends who have comprehensive plans and admire their drive. You know the type. One of your friends wants to be engaged by 24, married at 25, first child at 26. You marvel at their level of detail, but most of what they wanted manifested, didn't it? And if they didn't get it, they had back-up plans. No judgment, just assessment. Anything that we truly value requires a plan, beloved. <u>Events are planned because they are special, but also to make sure things happens.</u> Why wouldn't we give that same attention to our lives?

I'm not saying everything you do has to be scripted, but the journey is much better with a GPS. The problem is that it can only take us where we tell it to go. If we don't know or we keep changing the destination, how can we get there? I know we wake up and sit on the edge of the bed, before the day gets started. We shake our heads in wonder of where our lives went. How fast time is moving. Just yesterday you were a college or high school student with your entire life before you. Now you are waist deep in bills, kids, family drama, you name it. Many of us grew up with parents that handled everything. Now they are gone and our children look to us for guidance. What do we do?

Sit down with pen and paper; make a list of things you'd like to accomplish this year. If you're feeling ambitious, break it in to columns, long term and short-term goals. Make your goals as daring as you want. All you have to do is look at them every morning after you wake up and every evening before you go to bed. Your internal GPS will handle the rest. I promise you will feel better about YOU. Life is better when you know where you're going. When you and your partner have both answered the key questions about your life, are sure of your purpose and are actively working toward being your highest selves, you have fulfilled the first requirement of Relationship Equality. Have a plan!

What does a good relationship look like?

Before we go forward, let's go back to the beginning. The purpose of a relationship is to discover our true self. We learn about ourselves: likes, love and areas that need upgrading, through being with others. This other person is often called a counterpart, in the case of marriage, a spouse. I find these terms to be important.

The dictionary defines counterpart as a person or thing closely resembling another, especially in function. Isn't that how we partner with potential friends and lovers? We like them because they closely resemble us. The "Just Like Me" factor. I bet you've known friends or couples that were so close they finished each other's sentences, right? They move and think alike. In weights we call it a counter balance. So two key components of elevated unions are:

1. **LIKE ME** – Similar values, habits, morals and traditions.

2. **FOCUS** – Working on purpose with a balanced respect for self and others.

Being together should feel natural. In short, they should treat us as we would lovingly treat our self. They should treat us in the same fashion. It's the duality that shapes true Love. We are individuals; we are one.

What does this kind of relationship look like? It looks like two people on purpose, supporting each other's growth, keeping each other balanced, focused when one gets off track due to the siren song of this money mad world. This is a couple who will actively serve each other, their community and world in reaching the highest good and creating powerful families that will do the same.

What is the purpose of marriage?

Marriage is two people uniting in purpose, agreeing to support each other in pursuit of their highest form. Highest form does not mean accepting that someone is going to sit on the couch, watching TV and drinking beer for the next thirty years. It does NOT mean accepting mediocrity. It does not mean having an okay union.

The highest means the absolute pinnacle for self, union and family. It means that we see the divine spark in each other and agree to shepherd, guide, support, teach, encourage and wage war to protect that energy until it enlightens the world then returns to the source from which it came. To make that energy live again, for future generations through children, individuals with their own light, life, truth and purpose.

By having children, we intend to send products of our Love and Purpose to future generations with a promise of creating a more brilliant, loving world. I bet you never heard that in someone's vows. Relationships, at the point of equality, are an act of revolution. Wait, before the government knocks on my door, let me clarify that statement.

Relationships follow one of the dictionary's social definitions of revolution, which means a sudden and complete change in a procedure or course, as if in a circuit, back to a starting point. Some have supported the theory of life as being linear, meaning we start at one point then end at another. Straight line. I believe life is circular:

CIRCULAR LIFE: Harmonious Life

1. We are born in Love.
2. We are taught our beauty and power.
3. We discover and embrace our power.
4. We use that power to benefit others.
5. We discover our counterpart. (Love)
6. We combine power, light the world and ourselves.

7. We have offspring born in Love. Having lived, we return to our source.

LINEAR LIFE: Anxious Life

1. We are born in Fear.
2. We are taught to fear the world.
3. We fill our voids with recreation/diversion.
4. We chase money, power and things.
5. We find a mate attractive.
6. We fill our voids with each other's events. (PEA)
7. We have offspring born in fear. We die never having lived.

Children: The Best Part

When Love manifests, you feel it in every action. The vibrations of harmony buoy your mate and yourself. You feel as if nothing is impossible. You are correct. When this type of harmony or alignment is reached between couples, you have access to each other's physical, mental and spiritual power. Lovemaking is an action that gives juices the connection like the recharging a battery. Afterwards, you are not drained, but empowered.

The children, brought forth from this union, are full of purpose guided by divine influence. This is what we truly strive for in our unions. If we knew this power, we would never settle for anything less.

twenty

Life

The Duty and the Purpose!

There are two parts to every action we take in life. There is duty to and purpose for everything we do. Recognizing this is essential in living a meaningful life. So it is with the relationships we have with ourselves.

The relationship to self is the most important out of all in which we engage. It is, ironically, the one we neglect the most.

If we wish to have loving or Love filled relationship with others, we must first treat ourselves with that love. Love is like a house. No matter how well you decorate it, without a firm foundation, it will eventually crumble. When thinking about your relationship with you, keep the following in mind:

MY DUTY: To treat myself with respect, morality and obedience.

This means: I will honor my body mind and spirit with moral conduct in obedience to the creator and the energy that called me into being. I will not take actions against my physical, mental or spiritual well-being.

MY PURPOSE: To become the best me, possible.

This means: I will listen to my inner voice and allow myself to reach the height designed for me by my creators.

How many of us feel this way about ourselves? Do we love and honor our being, in all that we do? Or do we see our life as a struggle day to day with no passion for anything or featuring low energy?

I speak with people all the time who desire fulfilling relationships with others, which is wonderful. Then I ask them about themselves. They tell me they are in jobs they hate, have draining health issues and friends who constantly betray them. Well, I humbly suggest to them that before they start planning, they should seal and heal personal Voids.

It is our responsibility to see that we treat ourselves in a manner that honors our purpose. It is not up to someone else to do it for us, nor can we find it in PEA. Some would say that they feel okay about themselves, so what is the harm in that?

The people we call into our lives will treat us in line with the blueprint for duty and purpose we have set for ourselves. In short, if you feel "okay" or mediocre about yourself, you will attract someone who will give you okay treatment. Is that what you truly desire?

Duty and purpose to self will become your Life Treatment Blueprint. It will outline in great detail your expectations regarding conduct toward yourself by you, as by others. Anyone or anything not in harmony with these guidelines will be disallowed in your life. This is because you truly LOVE you.

twenty-one

Dating

How Long is the Test Drive??

In the modern world, dating is known at courtship or the time we set aside to find out if there is a future in a relationship. Whether it is serious dating or sport dating the eternal question is present, "Do you like me?" Recognizing that we all have Voids, the more important question is, "Do I like me?"

Dating nowadays is sloppy, unstructured and fails to achieve its true purpose and duty. Let's examine it:

What is Dating?

PURPOSE: Evaluation. To become familiar with a person.

DUTY: Assessment of characteristics befitting of a potential mate.

Isn't that simple? How do we manage to make that so complicated?

The purpose of dating is evaluation, plain and simple. To become familiar with a person is to get to know them. As outlined in an earlier chapter, it should be a thorough knowledge. We need to know what we are getting into.

The duty or obligation involved in dating is to assess. Are we compatible based on our likes, dislikes, habits and hates? Any man who has ever had a boy/man sniffing around his daughter or a mother who has had a girl/woman at her son's door has entertained this thought. Are they good enough for my baby? It depends on your evaluation.

If we take the word familiar from the purpose of dating then examine it closely, it provides the formula for the entire evaluation process.

Familiar is taken from the Latin, familia, which means household. The word famul, which means servant or slave, is also listed as a root. I take this to mean a familiar would be a person who is also a servant to the household or family.

Another definition for the word familiar gives the words, domesticated; tame. A person who is compatible with leadership. To sum it up, the ideal mate for your son/daughter would have obligations to the household, the larger family and need to be compatible with the elders of the family.

In days gone by, if the family didn't give their blessing, there could be no union between the couple. They recognized that the person was marrying the family as well. Those days are long gone.

In modern dating, many times, the family doesn't even meet the potential suitor until the relationship has been consummated. It may have been going on for several months or years. The family is expected to meet/greet the person, be nice and give their blessing. Oh, and then pay money if it becomes a marital situation. The negative side of familiar means a person too intimate, too personal, presumptuous and taking liberties. Which of these definitions sounds like your in-laws?

You see the danger? Modern dating is a way for Void Fillers to sniff out voids, exploit them all the while avoiding any type of evaluation. Family members don't get to see him/her and the person "dating" doesn't know who they are dealing with because they are given little to no information to go on. I've had women tell me that they don't know their boyfriend's last name. Come on. This is totally outside the purpose and the duty of dating. The other person might as well be invisible.

In the olden days, dating was called courting, which took place in a controlled environment. Safeguards against prejudice were implicit in the evaluation. Prejudice? Nothing skewers evaluation for a man or woman like the power of sex. We give passes to people who shouldn't have been allowed in the front door because we have already physically bonded with them. It is impossible to get a proper, non-biased reading once a couple has been intimate. In order to take effective action, we must recall purpose and duty in all of our relationships.

We can do this very easily by remembering the goal. Oneness with self, oneness with others, oneness with the creator or whatever energy to which you subscribe.

The family is supposed to be the platform supporting the mental, physical and spiritual development of individuals in ushering in a wonderful future generation that will create a better world.

In order to avoid the pitfalls of Dating in the Void, we must use the power of evaluation within the family. Dating is evaluation, not invitation. Dating will reveal most Voids. Pay attention to what you expect/feel you didn't get from your emotional pillars. Recognize where it comes from, address it and regain that power.

DO YOU OR YOUR MATE HAVE:
1. ABANDONMENT ISSUES
2. TRUST ISSUES
3. FAMILY ISSUES
4. MONEY ISSUES
5. BODY IMAGE/HAIR ISSUES
6. EMOTIONAL BAGGAGE
7. CHILD BEARING/CARING ISSUES

What issues does your date bringing to the table? They must be sorted through and addressed with plans on how to overcome the affects of each.

The power of attraction should be to their spirit, not from your vision. What vision perceives will fail, what the heart is attracted to is eternal.

Money goes, body goes and all we are left with is the alignment between our spirit and theirs. It is truly all that we have. Date with the highest purpose and duty. Evaluations are not invitations.

twenty-two
Parenting

Do the Best Job You Can With What You Know!

Your parents didn't screw you up on purpose. Once you read this book, please don't knock down your emotional pillars. They are there for a reason, to help you learn, to help you grow. Recognize that your parents did the best they could with what they knew, at the time. The fear they instilled, in you, was their own. The love they gave you was all that they had to give. What's done is done. However, recognizing what was done to you so you don't have to live it or pass it on to your children is wise. Reveal it, heal it, and seal it.

Reveal/recognize what was done to you, meaning its emotional affect. How it made you feel then, why you still feel that way. Heal what was done to you. Face the fear, speak its name and push through it. Your healing is on the other side. Once you overcome it, you will get all of your power back. Seal it.

Let's not ever go back to the things that held us hostage. Speak positive energy into all of your life. Say the thing and you will have the power. Pronounce the death of your fear; move forward in your journey.

Parenting has its purpose and duty like all of our actions.

PARENTING:

PURPOSE: To create a better world through enlightened people.

DUTY: To create a powerful, confident, loving child, as a part of a nurturing family in service to productive communities.

In short, our duty is to assist children in manifesting the power inside of them. To help them reach their highest point or the best version of themselves.

A child should be intelligent, sensitive, inquisitive and emotionally secure. They shouldn't fear a physical response from their parents as much as their disappointment. A child's actions should be in line with their moral intelligence. This does not require a ton of money, just time. When we spend quality time with children it makes them feel valued. This is the key to their security. We must model the qualities we wish to see in our children. Young people appear to not pay attention to their elders while the opposite is true. They pay attention to everything we do, most of what we say.

We mustn't let parental disagreements get in the way of our duty as parents. I am a child of divorce. My father left the household when I was very young. While I missed his presence in the house, what I really wanted was to spend time with him. This created one of the Voids I carried for years.

It still impacts me to this day. Why didn't he want to spend more time with me? Was there something wrong with me? Did I do something or not do something? Was I good enough?

These are the Voids that cripple many of us. Time and attention is all that is required to ensure that our wonderful children become well-adjusted adults. It is the key to making this world a better place. Children need to know three things to be secure:

CHILDREN NEED TO FEEL/KNOW:

1. HOW WAS I BORN? Circumstances?
2. WAS I DESIRED? Wanted?
3. WHY AM I HERE? Purpose?

It is that simple to make a child feel secure. They want to know the funny story associated with their birth. Tell them. My mother shared her story of going to the hospital to give birth to me. Her pregnant girlfriend drove her. The hospital workers mistakenly thought her friend was giving birth and not my mother. I have never forgotten that. Or my mother sharing with me that Dr. King was killed the month after I was born and everyone was sad, but she was happy to have her little boy. I know how I was born and that I was desired. That became my emotional foundation.

We must sit with our children and tell them. Helping children discover their purpose requires that we watch and expose. We must expose our children to different cultural, athletic and cognitive experiences then watch what they gravitate towards.

All children are born with gifts to assist humanity in becoming better. We must introduce them to new experiences, such as travel. They should see how other cultures live, witness the beauty of art, science and history.

To children, time is Love. Give it to them.

twenty-three

Ugly

IT'S IN YOUR MIND!

"God don't make ugly."
— *Grandma*

Good looks have nothing to do with good relationships. I've listened to women talk about other women who are successful in life, because of being commercially beautiful. I tell them that women and men are motivated by looks, to a point, but they are not the end game.

When one understands Void Thinking, they understand that there are two types of people in the context of relationship. Those striving to fill their voids in search of the "good" in life and those working with their gifts to fulfill their purpose.

In the case of attraction, men will be attracted to physical features without a doubt. But in the area of choosing a partner for a long-term relationship, it is more important to be in tune with the person on the level of their purpose. A level that will never fade. Looks, money and things will lose their attraction. The only enduring part of life is the spirit in which we live it.

STEPS TO GETTING & KEEPING ANY WOMAN/MAN YOU CHOOSE:

1. BE SURE THEY ARE WORTH IT.
2. BE ON YOUR LIFE PURPOSE.
3. EMBRACE THEIR LIFE PURPOSE.

I tell women all the time, if you want to get a good man and keep him, how you look has nothing to do with it. Neither does your financial status. Your **focus** has everything to do with it. First, make sure the man or woman is worthy of the effort. Then, be on your purpose in life. Finally, determine if your purposes coincide in a way that you can embrace each other. This will include mutual inspiration, motivation and perseverance.

Believe that you can have any man that you desire, knowing that it is pointless to play games, subvert how you truly feel or think like him in order to trick him into believing you are the one. You must be the one for **you.** Anyone you deem as worthy for the benefit of your love must be the one for **them.**

I've known women and men that have been in awe of their mates in college, only to be repulsed by how they look after children, lack of activity and filling their voids with food. What then? Do you leave the person because you are no longer attracted to them?

At the outset of the relationship, be sure that you are attracted to something that can never change. Something that will become more wonderful over time and that is a beautiful, warm, kindhearted, giving, spirit. The bling, the cars and the houses will fade with time, but the purity of a good spirit will endure.

TO GET ANY MAN/WOMAN YOU MUST:

1. KNOW/LOVE THE PERSON THEY ARE.
2. KNOW/LOVE THE PERSON THEY WANT TO BECOME.

Sounds simple because it is. It all revolves around knowing and understanding (loving) the person about whom you care. If you want to be in their life, make sure they are in it first. Then provide them with understanding. Nothing they wish to talk about should be off limits, especially when it relates to their past.

People have been through beautiful and terrible situations. They pray that someone will come along and understand them, listen to them without harsh or any judgment. **Be that person in truth, not to play a game.** Listen to them; let them know that it is all right. Create a safe zone in which you both reside.

Praise the person for having accomplished much and encourage them to go the rest of the path toward self-discovery. **Note:** I said self-discovery and not who you would like them to become.

You want the person to be in touch with self completely, no matter what that means. You must be willing to, at all times, sacrifice the US for the YOU. Simply put, if I want you to be happy, I understand that it means you might have to leave me to find it. Self-sacrifice is love's highest form when the self is truly valued. Then it is a true sacrifice.

Looks have nothing to do with relationships, because the most important is the one that a person carries on with self. That relationship dictates what we want/need to feel about self and the world around us. If you're the person who is able to meet that need, in truth, nothing else matters.

One of my favorite comedy films is "Shallow Hal," in which a guru hypnotizes the main character to only see the inner beauty of people. This causes commercially attractive people to become unattractive and vice versa. Hal discovers that looks don't matter in the face of people connecting spirits.

This could be easily compared to water, which we all need to live. Whether you get it from Poland Spring or the garden hose, it's still water. In other words, where we get it is a matter of taste, which is a matter of choice.

When we arrive at a place of true enlightenment, we will discover that the only truth is what we give to others from our spirit. Time or too much Haagen-Dazs can destroy anything else. If we truly care about someone, we owe him or her much more. I once believed that affection was the lynchpin of all great relationships, but now I know that was a mistake.

We cannot be filled by external things, but from the fountain of our own spirit. And if we need to share that spirit we can. But it must come from a place of abundance, not desperate need to fulfill the conditions of this world. The FEAR that tells you that you must be: married, employed, baptized or have children to be successful. The only thing you truly need is to be inspired by the life that you choose to live. What we like to feel is listed below.

WHAT WE LIKE TO FEEL:

- Secure
- Truthful
- Unique
- Understood
- Valued
- Purposeful

twenty-four

Life

*"It Isn't What You Think,
It's What You Think."*

— *D.W. Leonard*

One of my students asked me what LIFE is? I told her, "Life isn't what you think, it's what you think." Yeah, that's the same look she had on her face. I sincerely believe that people confuse Life with our modern reality. Life is in us, surrounds us. It is energy. Reality is our perception of that energy.

Because your thoughts determine your reality, it is up to you to set goals for your movement through those perceptions. With that in mind, to me, the only logical goal for Life would be connection or alignment. This is taking the time to make sure the Life the creator gifted us with is recognized as the wonderful energy it was meant to be, unclouded by muddy thoughts of lack and want.

One person works a 9-5 thinking it is the worst thing in the world. The other works the same job, happy to be there. They become a little ray of light in the office. Why the difference? PERCEPTION. You've heard it a million times. Your view is what shapes what you are seeing because you're not just watching, you're judging.

So why aren't we all the peppy person in the office? The Voids drain us, poison our thoughts with negativity against self and the world. So our reality becomes murky. Things that were plain to us in childhood, the joy of playing together, laughing together, become difficult to see. A spiritual book, don't want to prejudice you by telling you which one, states that goal of Life is, "The Perfect Purification of the Soul." I used to be a bitter, angry man. I would have scoffed at a guru claiming that gibberish a few years ago. Now I see the truth in these words.

We exist; go through problems, worries, pitfalls, and diseases in order to bring us into our perfect state. It's the pressure, often the pain that alters our being. Not pain in the punitive sense, but pain necessary to bring forth Life, as in child bearing. Though mothers don't like it, there couldn't be new life without it. Pain precedes benefit.

After revealing, healing and sealing our voids, the rush of Life should come back to us. The knowledge that each day is indeed our Birthday, a Holy Day to be celebrated because we are alive we have choice and can steer ourselves in whatever direction we choose, to wax Dr. Seuss.

Some people are able to achieve this wonderful transformation before they pass from this plane; others take the goal with them on their eternal journey. I believe all will become perfect because it is within us. Some people are angry, prejudiced adults but kindly elderly folks. What happened? Well, I believe that they witnessed the miraculous passing of time in this Life. It changed them.

Because they have slowed down, they can see the good in children, men and women of all races. Because they have stopped judging, they can see people struggling in areas where they themselves once toiled. Some people fear it, but growing old has a beauty all its own. It is truly a miracle.

Many of us worry about amassing fortunes, during our lives. We want to be rich more than anything else, so we kill ourselves with ridiculous work hours to achieve a little financial prosperity. If we were wise we could see that there is a Moral Wealth to life, which is not dependent upon income. Doing right by others for the sheer sake of good. Neither fearing consequence, nor seeking reward. Good for goodness sake.

Moral Wealth passed on to our children has the power to save future generations. Praise is vanity, but good deeds endure.

When my grandfather passed away, I was loading boxes out of his house. A man I'd never seen before, got out of his car and approached me. He told me how kind hearted, loving my grandfather had been to him. I received that Moral Currency. I treasure it to this day.

Money comes then goes, but the good we do for each other is everlasting. Until we are blessed to be together again:

Be good to yourself.

Be good to others.

BE INSPIRED!

D.W. LEONARD

Hardcore
Life
Blueprint

In order to get in touch with the Love within, create a journal and answer these questions as honestly as possible. The information is for you to examine your Hardcore Love Patterns and not for others to judge you. Your journal is for your eyes only.

1. What is your Life Purpose? (What have you been put here to do?)
2. Make a list of your talents/abilities.
3. What is your gift? The thing you do the easiest and best. It flows naturally.
4. What is your current occupation? Why? (Passion or pay bills)
5. How do you spend the majority of your time? Why?
6. What do you do as a hobby?
7. What do you hate for people to do to you and around you? Why?
8. If you were given one million dollars, what is the first thing you would do?
9. What do you love most about yourself? Explain in detail.
10. What is your best physical feature? What is your worst feature? Why do you say that?
11. What is your most valued possession? Why?
12. What is your dream occupation?
13. Are you working toward your dream? How?
14. What condition/ situation do you fear the most? Why?
15. Make a list of your 7 Emotional Pillars.
16. What did you give them?
17. What did you expect to receive?

18. What did you receive?
19. How did that make you feel about yourself?

In each category, there is a pattern of behavior that repeats itself. You will discover the forces that shaped you, when you are able to recognize the pattern. The pattern of expectation and disappointment or fulfillment made you into the person you are, especially in the area of Love. You were filled up or Voids were created. If my emotional pillars told me that I wasn't a priority, then I will seek a Love to reinforce that belief.

A. How did you handle conflict situations (fights) as a child? Do you still use the same method?
B. What expectations (if any) were placed on you in return for Love or Praise? Ex. You have to get good grades.
C. Do you still seek people to fill the same roles as your relationship pillars? Are you aware of your Love Patterns?

Part III – Honesty

1. What do you lie about the most? To yourself? To others? Why do you think this is necessary?
2. Does lying get you what you want?
3. How long are you willing to be dishonest about who you truly are and what you really want?

Attraction

4. What do you find most attractive about a person?
A. Physically? (Body)
B. Mentally? (Mind)
C. Socially? (Communication)
D. Spiritually? (Beliefs)

5. Which out of the four, listed above, is most important to you? Why? Explain.

Part IV - Revelation

6. When you meet someone, what is the first thing you want to know about him/her? (Besides their name)
7. What is the first thing you want them to know about you? Why?

8. What is the thing you hope to hide from them as long as possible? Why? (Please be detailed)

Part V – Desire

9. On a ratings scale of (1 – 5) how important is sexual intercourse to you? Why?
10. Describe your first sexual experience or sensual touch.
11. How did you feel about it at that time? How do you feel about it now?
12. Without being touched, what images stimulate you? Is there a connection between your first touch and those images?
13. What were the first images you witnessed as a child?
14. Is there a difference in your mind between sex and intimacy? What is the difference?
15. Have you ever considered your life without having children of your own? How did you feel? Why?

Part VI – Commitment

16. Has someone ever cheated on you in a relationship? Describe it. How did it make you feel?
17. How did that event change how you currently deal with relationships?
18. Do you expect people to always be honest with you?
19. If someone truly loves you, should they do whatever you say? Explain.
20. Have you ever lied about what you want/need in a relationship? Why?
21. Do you tell people exactly what you want, in a relationship, and then expect to receive it? What do you want? Did you receive what you now desire from your 7 Emotional Pillars?

Part VII – Obey

22. In a relationship, is it more important to obey your partner or your inner voice? Explain.
23. If you don't obey the people that love you, what will happen? What makes you think that? Explain.
24. If your partner doesn't obey you, do you punish them in some way? Why?
25. Is it your expectation that gifting those whom you love obligates them to you? Should they express gratitude? In what way?

26. Can you change your mind and change partners without feeling guilty? Why? Why not?

27. If someone breaks up with you, do you want him or her to be hurt by Karma and then apologize to you? Explain.

28. If your partner has sex with someone else, does that end the relationship as far as you are concerned? Why?

29. Would you listen to the reason for infidelity? Explain.

30. Could you ever trust a partner after they had sex and/or were intimate with another person? Why? Explain.

31. Does sitting with someone in a parked car constitute cheating in your opinion? Why?

32. Can a person cheat on their partner without having intercourse? Explain.

33. Which is more damaging to a relationship? Physical affairs or Emotional affairs? Explain.

Part VIII – Respect

34. How big a part has guilt played in your relationships as a child? Did your mother or father use guilt to get you to do their will? Explain.

35. Can you recall an incident when you gave love or sex to someone because you felt guilty?

36. Has guilt over what you did to or with a person ever caused you to stay in a non-elevating relationship? Why?

37. On a scale of (1 – 5) how great a factor are your parent's wishes on your life decisions?

38. On a scale of (1 - 5) how great a role do the opinions of your friends play in your decision-making?

Part VIIII – Equality

39. Do you have a plan for the development of your relationship or do you just go with the flow? Explain.

40. What is the purpose of your relationship with your partner? Does it have one? Explain.

41. How important is for your partner and yourself to like the same things and share the same focus? Why? Explain.

42. Do you have a duty to your partner? What is it? Explain.

Part X – Hardcore Life – Circular or Linear?

Answer each question with as much detail as possible.

1. Describe your parents' life together? If a single parent raised you, describe their life. What did they do everyday? Were they filled with joy or did they go through the motions? How did they function in their relationships?

2. How did your parents deal with bullies or conflict? Did they face it head on or wait for it to pass? Did they teach you to fight or get an adult to rescue you? Did they rescue you from consequences or let you feel the weight of your actions? How did that make you feel?

3. How do you think their conflict resolution style impacted the way you now deal with conflict?

4. How did your parents deal with pressure? Did they party or drink to excess? Did they use recreational drugs while encouraging you to live drug free? How did that make you feel?

5. How did you family deal with the topic of race? Were their opinions bigoted? Did they encourage you to treat everyone fairly or be wary of certain groups? How do you handle race as an adult? Do you teach your children the same?

6. How did you parents deal with money? Did they teach you to manage it or spend it? Was money available to you or scarce? How do you handle your own money? Do you treat it as a tool or something of which you will never have enough?

7. Did your parents ever ask you to lie? If so, in what situation? How did that make you feel? Have you carried that feeling into your adult relationships? Have you ever lied in that same situation? Explain.

8. Sum up your parents' Life Message into one sentence. Life is…

9. What is your Life Message? Life is…

10. Did your parents compliment your beauty? Your intelligence? Which did they praise the most? How did that make you feel? Do you still feel that way?

11. At what age did you discover what you wanted to be or do? Have you discovered it?

12. How does your life purpose affect how you view the world around you? Do you act locally or globally? Do you think mostly about the world or your own life? Why?

13. How is your partner's life similar to yours? Make a list.

14. What is the common goal of your relationship? What do you intend accomplish together? Have you discussed it?

15. Do you plan to have children? Toward what purpose? Have you discussed this with your mate?

16. Would you raise your children in the same manner in which your parents raised you? Why or why not?

17. What did your parents fear?

18. What did your parents teach you to avoid? Why?

19. List your habits, hobbies and hates and that of your parents. Make note of your similarities.

20. Is your partner attractive? Does that mean something to you? Were your parents attractive?

21. Did your partner's looks and education play into your friends/family approval or disapproval of them?

22. What do you believe is the most important message to deliver to your children? Explain.

Note: Take time to collect yourself, emotionally. Review all of your answers, carefully. Look for patterns, similarities between things your parents did or thought that carried over into your current behavior. Give special attention to how your emotional pillars handled conflict or dealt with disappointment. Think about their dreams for you or lack thereof. Think about how they lived their lives and how you currently live your own. Ask yourself, is this the way you intend to continue your life or is change necessary for you achieving your highest self?

If your desire is to change your life, know that you need to take action. It will not happen without your belief and effort. Know that it will not be easy, but it will be easier than you think and you will feel worlds better than you do now. Be patient with yourself, but know that you have to move. Quit that job, that spouse and whatever situation that reinforces the improper belief about yourself. Break-up with anything that says that you are less than, not good enough or second rate. Know that you are the best, the brightest and the only YOU on this planet. There will never be another. I love you, now you must love yourself.

D.W. Leonard